THE AGE OF CARS

THE
AGE
OF
CARS

MIKE TWITE

Hamlyn
London · New York · Sydney · Toronto

Acknowledgments: the publishers are grateful to the following for the illustrations reproduced in this book: Alfa Romeo; *Autocar*; Automobile Manufacturers Association; British Leyland Motor Corporation; Chrysler; Citroen; Briggs Cunningham Automotive Museum; Deutsches Museum; Eric Dymock; Fiat; Ford; Henry Ford Museum; General Motors; Martin Gross; Gulf Oil Corporation; Hispano-Suiza; David Hodges; Indianapolis Motor Speedway; Jaguar; Mercedes Benz; *Motor*; National Motor Museum; Philadelphia Free Library; Porsche; Radio Times Hulton Picture Library; Renault; Peter Roberts; Rolls-Royce; The Science Museum; Shell Photographic Service; Jasper Spencer-Smith; Smithsonian Institution; Nigel Snowdon; Mike Twite; Volkswagen; David Burgess Wise.

Published by The Hamlyn Publishing Group Limited
London · New York · Sydney · Toronto
Hamlyn House, Feltham, Middlesex, England
Copyright © The Hamlyn Publishing Group Limited 1973

ISBN 0 600 31759 5

Printed in England
by Sir Joseph Causton and Sons Limited

629.2
TWI

1. Automobiles

£

629.22
TWI
copy 1

CONTENTS

FROM CARRIAGE TO CAR

It is a strange paradox that we probably know as much about the Roman invasion of Britain before the birth of Christ as we do about the invention of the motor car. Quite why this should be is in itself a mystery, because one would imagine that the sound of an internal combustion engine would reverberate noisily in an age when one of the few sounds on roads was the clip-clop of horses' hooves. The truth is that many men were experimenting with horseless carriages, each taking a different approach to the problem; this engineer using steam, another electricity, and still others utilising the gas engine. With literally hundreds of people working on this problem it is not so surprising that the precise beginnings of the automobile are shrouded in mystery.

Our school history books used to tell us that James Watt invented the steam engine, that Karl Benz invented the motor car, that Alexander Graham Bell invented the telephone, that Orville and Wilbur Wright invented the aircraft, and so on. It was all neatly categorised, for no teacher wished to confuse children's minds with a mass of conflicting detail, and certainly not to admit that they were not certain who did invent what. Even today, the Russians and Chinese are claiming that they invented many things, including the car, and history books published in Germany, France and England give such widely differing views of historical events that the reader is led to wonder if they are even describing the same event.

Perhaps the most significant fact about the horseless carriage is that it was so long in coming.

For centuries men had realised the power of water and steam but no one was able to harness this energy to drive a vehicle. So the only means of transport available to man until the nineteenth century was the horse-drawn vehicle and the sailing boat. Even when the car was seen to be a viable proposition there were many people who sought to restrict its use, and who could only view the motor car as a toy — among them, it might be added, a number of car constructors. The aircraft suffered a similarly troubled birth at the beginning of the twentieth century.

The motor car of today can trace its beginnings back to the early eighteenth century, when the stationary steam engine was invented. James Watt, who did not really invent the steam engine, perfected a design of Thomas Newcomen's for a stationary engine and set up in business building them, largely for use in mines where much water had to be pumped out of the workings. Development of steam engines then began to move rapidly both in Europe and North America, and although evidence is scanty it is generally recognised that a Frenchman, Joseph Cugnot, built the first full-size mechanically propelled vehicle in 1770. His three-wheeled vehicle was a tractor designed to tow artillery, the single front wheel carrying the boiler which pivoted with the steered wheel. The course of history might well have changed at this point, but Napoleon was busy elsewhere and took little notice of the revolution taking place in one of his arsenals. If development had been hastened by the exigencies of war, as recent history shows, who knows what victories Napoleon might have won, unhampered by the need to feed countless horses?

One of James Watt's workers, William Murdock, built a model steam carriage in about 1785 but it was not developed. Nor was the crude device built by Oliver Evans in Philadelphia in 1805, for a single self-propelled road journey, of any real significance. However, at about the same time, Richard Trevithick, a well known steam engineer, built a steam carriage which actually ran at its first attempt, although it was subsequently burnt out the same night while the inventor was toasting his success at a local inn! He built several more steam carriages and in 1808 brought one of them to London from Cornwall with the idea of attracting finance for his ventures, but he failed.

Over the next twenty or thirty years a large number of steam carriages were developed, many of them with fairly sophisticated boilers, but they were usually very large, cumbersome devices with little in the way of performance, steering or braking. Despite the handicaps, men like Goldsworthy Gurney, Charles Dance, Walter Hancock and W. H. James built workable machines, a number of which went into public service as coaches. But with mechanical problems still prevalent, high toll charges levied on steam vehicles and the rapid development of railways, the steam coach soon faded away. The growth of the railways tended to inhibit the development of road vehicles, for who would bother to buy and run a vehicle on the appalling roads of the mid-nineteenth century when he could ride in a smooth running train at less cost?

Although James Watt had initiated Britain's industrial revolution, and his sophisticated versions of Newcomen's engine mechanised much of industry, road transport still had to rely on the horse, because nobody was able to design and build a lightweight steam engine to propel a road vehicle, and it was left to other men to develop the motor car.

Experiments with gunpowder engines and hot air engines led nowhere and the first sign of a light, powerful engine came in 1824 when an Englishman, Samuel Brown, invented a gas engine using sulphuretted hydrogen, but this proved uneconomic and was abandoned. The next step came when the French engineer Etienne Lenoir developed a coal gas burning engine, which in principle was based on the steam engine. Although a version of this engine was fitted to a crude car which ran in 1862, it was hopelessly inefficient and wasteful of fuel. In the same year, the German engineer Nikolaus August Otto began experiments with a stationary gas engine with which he persisted for several years, until in 1867 he received a gold medal at the Paris Exhibition, and orders began to pour in, mostly from factories wishing to drive machinery and from mines for pumping work – in 1871 Otto and his backer, Eugen Langen, were forced to float a new company and find a bigger factory to cope with orders. An engineer named Gottlieb Daimler was hired to become Chief Engineer. Otto established the four-stroke principle, now known as the Otto cycle, which he and Daimler perfected and patented in 1876. Otto's earlier design, and indeed all other gas engine designs, had relied on atmospheric pressure and the piston's own weight to return it after the explosion, but he realised that by compressing the mixture before ignition he could obtain a much more powerful and smooth running engine.

As soon as the success of the Otto engine was demonstrated, rival and vested interests began to try to break the patents granted to it and after many court cases they finally won on the basis of a dubious engine which had been made by a man called Reithmann and by some notes prepared by a French engineer, Alphonse Beau de Rochas. Only in England was Otto's patent upheld by the courts.

Relations between Otto and Daimler became very strained and in 1882 Daimler was dismissed from the service of Gas Motoren Deutz. He then set up in business with Wilhelm Maybach and began to develop Otto's engine, using hot tube ignition instead of gas jet ignition. By 1885, they had greatly developed their four-

Early light steam carriages – Thomas Rickett's 1859 machine (*top*) and American Richard Dudgeon's steamer (*above*); an example still exists.
Below: Gottlieb Daimler's first four wheeled horseless carriage, built in 1886.

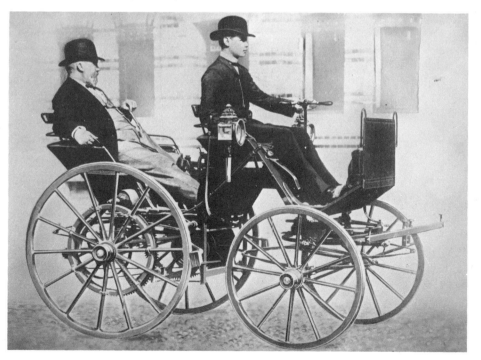

stroke engine, utilising benzine fuel instead of coal gas by means of a surface carburettor, and they set about applying it commercially. It was successfully used in a boat and in 1885 Daimler fitted an engine to a three-wheeled, wood-framed machine which was just capable of moving.

At the same time, however, another German, Karl Benz, was working on the motor car and in 1885 he too designed a four-stroke engine and fitted it to a three-wheeled machine. The engine was relatively sophisticated for that time, having mechanically operated valves, a surface carburettor, water cooling and trembler-coil ignition. With a capacity of 985 cc it gave three-quarters of a horse power, which was

barely enough to persuade the machine to move. The engine and the tricycle were rapidly developed, however, and by 1888 Benz was selling vehicles to the public, for by that time his engine gave 3 horse power and the tricycle could achieve 15 mph.

Benz can certainly be considered as the father of the motor car, insofar as he put the first viable car on the road and was able to sell it. Daimler followed suit in 1889 with a car which many people considered better than the Benz.

Suddenly, the floodgates were opened. Many of the people who had pooh-poohed the idea of a self-propelled vehicle rushed to produce copies of the Daimler and Benz models. The initiative passed from

Pioneer Henry Ford in his first car, built in 1896 (*above*). The rude mechanicals and the belt drive transmission of a Benz (*opposite, top*). The first American car was the Duryea (*right*), here with Charles Duryea at the wheel in 1895.

Germany to France and soon firms like Delahaye, Panhard et Levassor, de Dion and Peugeot were manufacturing cars in some quantities.

The horseless carriage was accepted slowly in England and it was left to a few pioneers to import French and German machines into what, at that time, was the most powerful industrial nation. In the United States of America the situation was little better. A charlatan named George Selden had managed to obtain a

8

patent on a petrol driven motor car in 1895, which meant that anyone wishing to build such a vehicle in the United States had to pay royalties to him. This they dutifully did until Henry Ford challenged the patent, finally winning his case in 1911 after a marathon eight year battle.

Automobile development thundered ahead, leaving Daimler and Benz far behind as thousands of brains tackled the many problems of perfecting the horseless carriage. By 1900 both Otto and Daimler were dead, but Benz lived to the age of 85 and when he died in 1929 he was feted and revered as the inventor of the motor car.

The credit for rescuing the car from its 'motorised dogcart' image must go to Emile Levassor of the Panhard et Levassor company. Most early cars had rear-mounted engines driving a rear wheel by belts, but Levassor mounted the V-twin Daimler-Phenix engine at the front, driving to the rear wheels through a friction clutch on the flywheel and then to a series of sliding pinions on a shaft mating with various gear wheels, the drive being taken to the dead rear axle by a single chain to the centre of the axle. Although it was a crude device, the Panhard of 1891 set the design trend for many years to come.

Next on the scene in France was the extrovert Comte Albert de Dion who, playboy though he was, saw the possibilities of the car and began working on a steam car with Georges Bouton. They eventually abandoned steam in favour of an internal combustion engine and designed a neat, high revving unit which ran twice as fast as the 750 rpm Daimler engine. This 1500 rpm unit necessitated the invention of positively timed ignition (of similar design to the mechanical contact breaker used today) and one more step had been made in automobile knowledge. That this engine is long lived is proved every November by the large numbers of de Dion Boutons which appear in the annual London to Brighton run for veteran cars. Later works manager Trépardoux invented the type of rear axle which bears de Dion's name, and which is in use on some production cars, such as Rovers.

In America, Charles and Frank Duryea built a car in 1893 and formed the first US car manufacturing company two years later (although Henry Ford had built an engine in 1893, he did not produce his first car until 1896). The crude Duryea machine holds a place in history because it won the first ever motor race held in America, but soon the firm faded into obscurity. The few cars which were available in America in the 1890s were mostly imported, and were hardly usable on the poor roads outside towns. America, at that time, had concentrated her energies on building railroads, at the expense of road development.

By the turn of the century France and Germany had well developed motor industries. Italy was just establishing one, the first Fiat being built in 1899, but the rest of Europe and America relied almost entirely on the few importers of foreign machines.

The reluctance of most people to accept the motor car was quite understandable. The cars were extremely noisy, slow, difficult to operate, unreliable, suffered many punctures during the period while pneumatic tyres were developed and perfected, and offered little weather protection for the driver and passengers. Since cars could cost upwards of £400 when a good average weekly wage was five shillings, these vehicles were very much for the wealthy.

In England, horseless carriage owners had to contend with a savage law, which was rigidly enforced. Prior to 1865, the law allowed light locomotives to travel at speeds of 10 mph outside towns, and 5 mph in towns. However, a law of 1865 reduced these speeds to 4 and 2 mph respectively, and also required that three people should be with any vehicle, one of whom had to precede it by at least 60 yards and carry a red flag. There were few road vehicles at that time and this law caused little hardship, but as cars began to appear in increasing numbers it caused endless trouble, with repeated prosecutions of early automobilists, as they were known. However, by 1896 the 'red flag law' had been repealed, and in that year the maximum speed was raised to 12 mph; the Motor Car Act of 1903 raised it to 20 mph. To celebrate the 1896 law an Emancipation Run was staged from London to Brighton, which at the time did little to aid the cause of the motor car, as only 10 of the 33 starters reached Brighton and some of them were

alleged to have made much of the journey by train, but has since been commemorated every November in the most famous of all historic car events.

Despite the slow and poor start made by the horseless carriage it quickly gathered patronage as more and more people realised its tremendous potential. Development leaped forward at an astonishing pace in the late 1890s and early 1900s, so much so that by the time the First World War started the layout of the car had reached a stage closely akin to that of present day machines. 'Horseless carriages' soon disappeared, and gave way to purpose designed automobiles. Belt drive gave way to side chains and chains gave way to the

Above: before Rolls. Henry Royce began building cars because he was dissatisfied with the quality of other cars. This one is a 1903 Royce.
Left: the start of the 1896 Emancipation Day run from London's Metropole Hotel in 1896. Harry J. Lawson is seen in the leading car, which was probably among those despatched by train to Brighton to ensure their safe arrival.

propeller shaft we know today, exposed bodies gave way to enclosed saloon bodies, tiller steering was soon abandoned in favour of wheel steering and solid tyres were very quickly replaced by pneumatic tyres.

France still set the pace, with Panhard, Peugeot, de Dion and Renault showing the world's automobile industry how it should be done. The German motor industry did not advance very rapidly, in part as Karl Benz tended to be complacent about his past achievements, refusing to develop the motor car any further. Therefore his dogcart-like machines soon became outdated. Britain was enmeshed in the machinations of an entrepreneur who, in today's more forthright language, would be termed a swindler. H. J. Lawson appeared on the English scene in 1895; to his credit he foresaw the importance of the automobile and began to buy up patents, whether they were worthwhile or not. He formed the Motor Car Club, the Daimler Motor Company and the Great Horseless Carriage Company, with plans to build a variety of cars for which he held licences, such as the de Dion, Daimler and Panhard et Levassor. Unfortunately, he and his co-directors were more interested in making

money than in building cars and very few vehicles ever left their factories. Instead, Lawson concentrated on trying to extract money from other people who were building cars in England. He alleged they were infringing his numerous patents, but development was moving so fast that most companies were able to avoid court action and Lawson lost all prominence. He had effectively delayed Britain's emergence as a motoring nation by five years or more; contrarily, he was one of the prime movers in organising the famous Emancipation Day run to Brighton.

An eccentric American inventor called E. J. Pennington came to England with an engine design which he sold to Lawson for £100,000 — a great deal of money at the turn of the century. The engine was entirely useless, as were all of Pennington's designs, and never powered a production car. Mr Pennington soon returned to America.

While Britain and America were floundering, European manufacturers were advancing rapidly. Motor racing, which had started in 1895, was becoming a spectacular proving ground for the motor car. The great town to town races attracted millions of spectators. However, in 1903 the Paris–Madrid race was stopped at Bordeaux by the French government because of the number of drivers and spectators killed in accidents — few people had suspected the carnage an uncer-braked, unstable 80 mph racing machine could cause on the dirt roads of the period. Motor racing was never quite the same again, but it had already proved an excellent test bed for French and German manufacturers.

CARS FOR CONNOISSEURS

Early in the twentieth century the world's motor industry fell into the pattern which was to last until the 1930s, building cars which at extremes ranged from simple cars for the masses to the costly, lavish and often beautiful cars built in small numbers for the nobility, or simply the rich.

One of the most significant early advances came in Germany with the introduction in 1901 of the Mercedes. This model resulted from the enthusiasm of Emil Jellinek, who was the Austro-Hungarian consul in Nice. Jellinek was not enamoured by the Canstatt-Daimler model which Maybach had designed (and for which he was agent in the South of France), so he persuaded Maybach to build a new model. This had a pressed steel chassis, the sort of honeycomb radiator we know today and a 35 hp engine fitted with mechanically operated inlet valves. This sophisticated car was christened Mercedes, after Jellinek's daughter, a name which remains in use today with Mercedes-Benz.

In the early 1900s, and until well into the 1920s, motoring was the perogative of the wealthy, who could afford the high purchase cost, ruinous running expenses and a chauffeur to drive and maintain the vehicle. Since tyres invariably punctured on the poor roads and mechanical breakdowns were expected as a matter of course, it often was not considered practical to drive oneself. Because the majority of cars had little or no weather protection the supply of special motor clothing became a new and thriving industry. The driver and passenger were usually enveloped in full length coats, the driver sporting a peak cap and goggles. Ladies wore

hats with long veils to protect them from the dust (some of these veils had a celluloid panel at the front so that the wearer could see where she was going). The difficulties did not end there, for garages were non-existent, spares could only be obtained from the factory and the local blacksmith would have to be called in for major repair work. Add to this the hostile attitude of the police and many members of the public and it is easy to understand why the motor car made slow progress, in Britain especially.

Gradually, as knowledge and experience of motor cars was consolidated, vehicles increased in size, an indication of the wealth of the owner, and leaving aside for a moment the small cars produced, the rich in their large cars began to motor in great comfort by the standards of the day.

Coachbuilders who had previously constructed horse-drawn carriages adapted their techniques to the needs of the car, firstly by building on car chassis bodies virtually identical to those they were building on horse-drawn vehicles. They soon realised the need for different bodies and the car body we know today was gradually developed. Car bodies largely consisted of a cover for the engine, a pair of armchairs for driver and front seat passenger and a settee for the rear seat occupants. Naturally everything was beautifully made, with seasoned ash forming the body structure and mahogany or other hard woods on the parts that were exposed. Trimming was carried out in heavily buttoned leather, and paintwork was applied in an incredibly laborious fashion, a typical body having six or seven undercoats, each sanded down, then a coat of stain, five or six top coats, each one sanded down, followed by six or seven coats of varnish, each one sanded down. Then elaborate coach lines and family crests would be added. This work could take weeks, but with low wages and men glad of the work the quality was high and the cost modest.

It is surprising that few people thought about such items as doors, windscreens or a roof, although all of these had existed on horse-drawn vehicles. The need to conserve weight was one reason, but few owners seemed to mind the exposure to the weather. But by 1905 these 'extras' were being fitted to cars, although the chauffeur was still expected to live out front, unprotected from inclement weather. The Cape Cart hood was in vogue for a time, and was a collection of fabric and hood sticks, far worse than the canopies of present-day convertibles, about which many drivers complain.

The Englishman's lot was eased slightly in 1903 when the speed limit was raised from 12 to 20 mph, but at

Above: brave British attempt to build a luxury tourer was made by Leyland with their eight cylinder car; only 18 were sold. Beloved by the Royal family for many decades, the Daimler marque reached its pinnacle with the sleeve valve Double-Six (*right*). This royal car, with typically conservative body, is posed outside Buckingham Palace.

the same time it became a legal requirement that all cars should be registered and fitted with a number plate, and the driving licence was brought into being — at an annual cost of five shillings.

By 1904 Britain's motor industry had begun to catch up with its counterparts on the Continent. British engineers such as Lanchester developed ingenious designs and cars were being produced in increasing numbers. It was estimated that around 9,000 cars were on British roads in 1904 and by the time the First World War started in 1914, no less than 130,000 vehicles were registered. Of course, these numbers were still quite small by comparison with today's vehicle registration figures, but since so few people were in a financial position to buy a car it was good progress.

Names that were to become famous emerged with the infant industry, such as Napier and Rolls-Royce. Napier did much to pioneer the six-cylinder engine, aided in no small measure by Selwyn Edge, whose flair for publicity would not disgrace a modern public relations

expert. Montague Napier's cars were excellent but it was Edge who made them a household name; his most notable triumph was gained on the newly opened Brooklands track in 1907 when he drove a 60 hp Napier for 24 hours at an average speed of 65 mph — quite a feat in those days (he was not thanked by the track's owner, Major Locke-King, because the Napier did a lot of damage to the new concrete surface). Certainly Napier was the premier British quality car for many years, until usurped by Rolls-Royce, but they carried on making cars until 1924 when car manufacture ceased in favour of the aero engine side of their business,

which was becoming equally famous. The big Napier Six of the 1906–1914 era was a quiet, good handling car of great refinement.

The story of Rolls-Royce is one of the most romantic in an industry not noted for sentiment. Henry Royce, an electric crane manufacturer, was not impressed by the quality of the imported motor cars he had seen, and designed his own. This did impress the Hon. C. S. Rolls, a leading figure in the new motoring, and he came to an agreement with Royce to form Rolls-Royce Ltd. Rolls was already selling Panhard cars in England but sales were declining and he was glad to sell the Rolls-Royce. The first

model to gain fame was the 7-litre 40/50 six-cylinder model of 1906, which was named the Silver Ghost. By the standards of the day the car was incredibly silent, the engine was extremely flexible and the fastidious Royce had eliminated many of the petty annoyances displayed by cars of the day. It quickly gained favour among connoisseurs, even though the bare chassis was priced at £985.

Rolls set about selling and publicity – in 1906 he won the Tourist Trophy race and broke the unofficial London–Monte Carlo record, before in 1910 he was killed in a flying accident at Bournemouth. In 1911 a Silver Ghost was driven from London to Edinburgh and back in top gear and in 1913 a team of Rolls-Royces won the Alpine Trial. Thereafter, the factory took no part in competition.

Rolls-Royce continue to build fine cars to this day, the current Silver Shadow following a succession of models with the first name of Silver, such as Silver Cloud and Silver Dawn. Another popular Rolls-Royce name was the Phantom, which is still in use (the latest Phantom being the VI).

Sir Henry Royce died in 1933, only two years after he had acquired the moribund Bentley company, and many stories, mostly apocryphal, grew up about the legendary reliability of the Rolls-Royce. Most of these stories are angled on the legend that Rolls-Royce are supposed never to break down, so that mechanics are allegedly flown all round the world with spare parts to repair cars and then inform the owner that there was nothing wrong with them. One true story is that Rolls-Royce never quote the horsepower of their engines; there is even a story about that, for one potential American customer is supposed to have cabled the factory to ask for details of the power output of the model in which he was interested. Back came the one word reply – 'Sufficient'.

The British Daimler firm, which was originally formed to build German Daimlers under licence, very early on decided to build their own cars under the guidance of F. R. Simms, to whom goes the credit for the term *motor car* – before that they had been known officially as light locomotives. In 1900, Daimler achieved the distinction of Royal Patronage when the Prince of Wales, later King Edward VII, bought a Daimler. Until the late 1950s, a Daimler was always included in the

The stately Rolls-Royce has always been the epitome of elegance but this Phantom 1 model surpassed them all. The interior is fitted out like an Edwardian drawing room using the most expensive woods, tapestries, curtains and other appurtenances of gracious living.

Top: American body builders constructed some notable bodies on Rolls-Royce chassis. This 1928 Phantom 1 is fitted with speedster phaeton coachwork by Brewster. The Hon. C. S. Rolls gained fame both in the motoring and aviation worlds. Here he is shown in a Silver Ghost Rolls-Royce with the Short brothers who were famous aviation pioneers – one of their machines is in the shed.

Royal household's fleet of cars. In 1909, Daimler, in search of the silence and smoothness of the Rolls-Royce Silver Ghost, developed an engine using the sleeve valve design of the American, Charles Knight. This form of valve gear was very silent but the engines were unable to develop much power and the cars were invariably trailed by a haze of blue smoke. Engines became vast, culminating in the twelve-cylinder 7-litre Double-Six model of 1927 and a series of straight eights. The big Daimler chassis was often fitted with some of the most extravagant bodies ever seen. Daimlers and Rolls-Royces were popular with Indian Maharajas who crammed the bodies with as much gold, silver and ivory decoration as the groaning chassis would support. The fortunes of Daimler began to decline in the depression of the early 1930s, and in 1960 the company was absorbed by Jaguar,

after a brief flirtation with a glass fibre bodied sports car.

W. O. Bentley was trained as a locomotive engineer, a fact which many of his detractors used against him because of the size and weight of most of his car designs. Ettore Bugatti, who designed some exquisitely light and fast machines, is supposed to have said of the 4½-litre Bentley which won the Le Mans 24 Hour race *"Le plus vite camion du monde"* — the fastest lorry in the world. Bentley designed a very successful rotary aero engine which gave good service during the First World War and is credited with developing the aluminium piston which overcame many of the problems of the piston engine. His first car, the 3-litre, was built in 1919 and followed by engines of increasing size, moving up to 4½-litres, 6½ and finally 8-litres. Bentleys were mostly fitted with open sports bodies of the 'Bulldog Drum-

mond' type but a number of attractive closed bodies were built on the chassis, especially the 6½ and 8-litre models. Unfortunately, Bentley did not last more than eleven years, but in that time the *marque* won the Le Mans race five times and probably more examples of the Bentley *marque* exist *pro rata* than any other make. As W. O. Bentley himself said when he reviewed a vast array of Bentleys at an owners club meeting, "There seem to be more here than we ever made, and most of them look in better condition than when we first turned them out!" The Bentley company was taken over by Rolls-Royce in 1931 and most Bentleys made since then have been largely modified Rolls-Royces.

It is often forgotten that Renault made 'voitures de grand luxe' in the 1930s, like this sedanca de ville.

The brass-bound splendour of a sporting 60 horsepower Mercedes, built in 1904. Ignition and throttle controls are on the steering wheel, gear and brake levers are side by side on the right, while ahead of driver and passenger is an oil reservoir and a battery of sight-feed lubricators for the four-cylinder engine.

A potential rival to Rolls-Royce was Hispano-Suiza, the Spanish builders of quality cars. Their designer was Marc Birkigt, a Swiss electrical engineer (hence the firm's association in the title, although in fact the company factories were in Spain and France). He began designing cars as early as 1901, and for Hispano-Suiza was responsible for a range of large chassis which quickly caught the attention of connoisseurs, including King Alfonso XIII of Spain. The H6B 37·2 model, designed and built at the Paris factory, was the car which made Hispano-Suiza's name. It featured a 6·6-litre aluminium engine with a single overhead camshaft. This gave 135 bhp and was capable of pulling a heavy car up to 85 mph very quic<ly, while a later 8-litre version called the Boulogne was capable of 110 mph. Not content with this 8-litre model, Hispano-Suiza developed a 9·4-litre V12 model which was easily capable of 115 mph in 1931,

Left: elephantine Mercedes. A 1930 example of the 'Grosser' Mercedes, fitted with an eight cylinder 7·7 litre 200 horse power engine. A Teutonic rival for the Mercedes was the V12 Maybach Zeppelin with an eight speed gearbox (*opposite*). A Franco-Spanish alliance produced the immortal Hispano-Suiza 37·2 of the late 1920s (*below*).

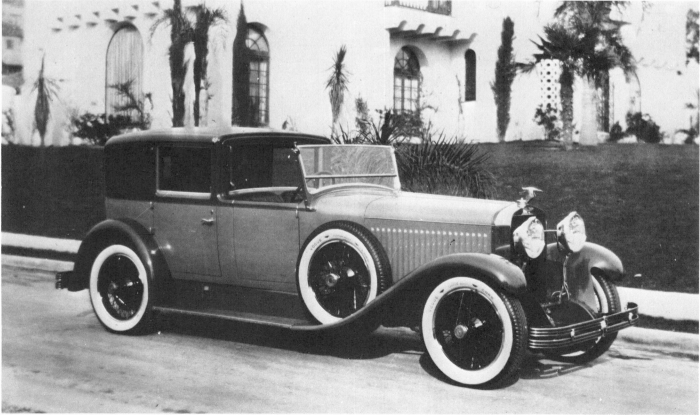

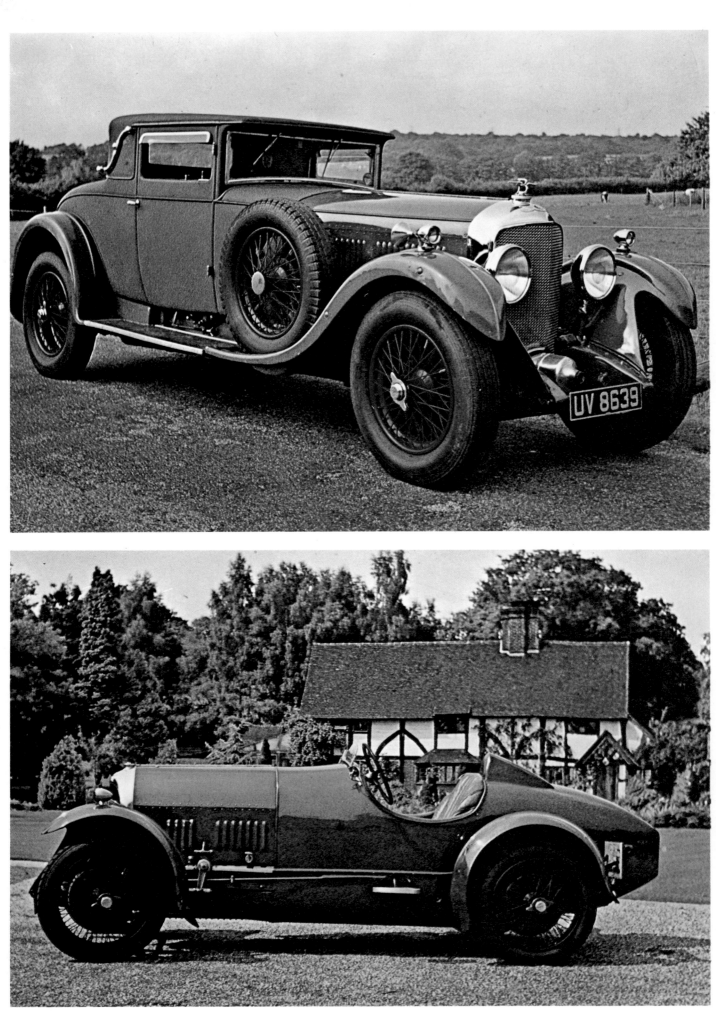

Opposite: one of the fine cars of the late 1920s was the Speed Six Bentley. This one (*top*) is fitted with a rather claustrophobic body built by Jack Barclay. Financier Woolf Barnato supported Bentley for many years, racing the 3-litre and 4½-litre cars with great success. He had this 3-litre car (*lower photograph*) specially bodied for him.

Above: a more formal type of body fitted to Rolls-Royce chassis was the sedanca-de-ville in which the chauffeur was exposed to the elements. This is a Phantom 1.

Left: a popular body style in the early days of motoring was the 'Roi des Belges' which consisted merely of four, luxurious armchairs, with no bodywork to speak of at all. This is a 1906 30 hp Mercedes.

at a time when most small cars could barely exceed 50 mph. Coachbuilders prized the honour of constructing their coachwork on these advanced chassis. One of the most famous bodies on the Hispano is a boat-tailed speedster entirely made from small planks of tulip wood riveted to a light metal framework.

In America, where the trend towards automobiles for the masses was much stronger than in Europe, the 'quality' car manufacturers did not flourish in such numbers, but many opulent cars were made, some beautiful, others vulgar. Among the classics

was the Auburn Speedster, which had a straight eight engine and a guaranteed 100 mph performance, personally checked by head tester, Ab Jenkins; it is now a much sought after model. The 'coffin nose' Cord 810 and 812 with V8 engine and front-wheel drive were fine cars which became popular with sportsmen. The Cadillac was the chassis to which the carriage trade looked, especially the V16 which could carry large saloon bodies and still perform respectably, since they would accelerate smoothly from a standstill to 90 mph in top gear.

Among the quality makers in America were Lincoln, Marmon, Pierce-Arrow, Packard, Ruxton and Stutz, all of whom built fine cars. Few survived the depression of the early 1930s and those that did were absorbed into larger organisations. Perhaps the most sought after Ameri-

Below: one of America's finest cars was the model J Duesenberg, invariably fitted with luxurious body-work. This one is a boat-tailed speedster. Stutz was another famous American make – this is one of the less exotic models (*bottom*).

Top: the 'coffin nose' Cord 810, now one of the most sought after American classics. Acclaimed as one of the great cars of all time, the 1935 V16 Cadillac (*above*) was capable of cruising at 100 mph.

can car is the Duesenberg, of which barely 500 were built. The best known model is the J, announced in 1928 featuring a straight eight 6·9 litre Lycoming engine, claimed to give 265 bhp. A later supercharged model was claimed to give 320 bhp and in sports trim was said to top 130 mph.

The Duesenberg was much prized by film stars and other notables who vied with each other to purchase lavish bodywork from the top coach-builders of the day, like Le Baron, Murphy and Judkins. Some truly beautiful cars were produced by Duesenberg and the surviving examples are quite rightly prized as collectors' pieces, fetching very high prices on the rare occasions they come up for sale.

There were many other quality *marques* which thrived in the age of elegance but gradually economic

factors forced them out of business. Few car enthusiasts who have driven these distinctive vehicles will forget cars like the Alfa Romeo 8C, the 8-litre Bentley, the Bugatti type 57SC, the Cadillac V16, the Daimler Double-Six, the Delage D8120, the SJ Duesenberg, the Isotta-Fraschini, the 37·2 Hispano-Suiza, the V12 Lagonda, the SSK Mercedes, the V12 Packard, the Rolls-Royce Phantom II, and the Stutz Bearcat. The age of elegance may have disappeared, but fortunately some of its cars survive to remind us of it.

MOTORS FOR MILLIONS

Although the motor car had begun to achieve fairly widespread acceptance in Great Britain by 1914, it was still largely the preserve of the wealthy. Whereas the general public could ride on omnibuses and have some of their goods delivered by motorised vans, few people were in a position to own a car. Even the armies of the First World War went to battle largely on horses or their feet, but motorised vehicles steadily came into more general use towards the end of the War. The oceans of mud on the battlefields of the Western Front were not suited to the use of wheeled vehicles, and even the newly-introduced tanks were not able to cope very well with the appalling conditions. During the war millions gained some mechanical knowledge and after it most wanted to become motorised; inevitably large numbers of small manufacturers sprang up to try and satisfy this need. Most were founded more on optimism than practical reality, and had very short lives. But Henry Ford had already shown the way ahead, and his example was followed by Austin, Citroen, Morris and Renault, who made real motoring for the masses possible.

For a brief period, the cyclecar flourished. This class of vehicle had been born in the years just before the war, for what might be termed the marginal motorist – the man who really should have bought a motorcycle but also wanted to provide transport for his wife. These devices were incredible in their crudeness – a typical example comprised little more than a simple steel or wood chassis, a pair of axles on leaf or coil springs, a twin-cylinder motorcycle engine driving the rear wheels by belts, steering by the sort of wire and pulley arrangement that would hardly be tolerated on a child's pedal car, and virtually non-existent brakes. If you were lucky you might get an aluminium body, but sometimes they were made of hardboard and indeed in one case the body was actually *papier-maché* which virtually dissolved if the owner was foolish enough to drive it in the rain! Most cyclecars would accommodate two people but some were single seaters, completely devoid of weather protection and other comforts.

The cyclecar boom did not last long because of the availability of 'real' cheap cars – above all the Model T Ford in America, which inspired several European firms to imitate Henry Ford's methods. Unfortunately, capital was in very short supply and even attempts by some firms to amalgamate their production facilities did not bring any marked success. With shortages of materials, labour disputes and so on, British manufacturers of 'proper' cars could not keep prices at an attractive level and any sort of reasonable small car cost around £500 in 1920. So the cyclecar at £100 or even less had a good, if short, innings.

In America the car developed much more rapidly than in Europe, and along different lines. The aim of manufacturers and public alike was to get everyone on wheels, so the builders concentrated on cars for the masses rather than for the wealthy.

Opposite top: **a selection of popular cars about to start a section on the Land's End Trial, and a JAP-engined Morgan driven enthusiastically in a 1933 trial.**
Right: **a 10·8 hp Riley Redwing of the mid-1920s.**

Road building was given greater priority in the States and the need for the car was more urgent. The ever lengthening railroads could not reach every corner of the North American continent.

Henry Ford, who had built various models which were mainly noted for their relative cheapness, decided in 1908 to build his new car, the Model T, on an assembly line basis, keeping the design unchanged for as long as the demand existed. In this way he was able to purchase large stocks of bought-out components at rock bottom prices and his assembly line process reduced building costs to a minimum.

The design of the model T was simple, yet the components were robust and the car rapidly gained a reputation for strength and durability. The four cylinder side-valve engine had a capacity of 2·9 litres, but only developed 22 bhp — the power was deliberately restricted by reducing in size the carburettor and inlet passages to gain reliability from an unstrained engine. The engine was built in unit with the two speed epicyclic gearbox and transmission brake while a splash lubrication system miraculously lubricated the whole assembly. The clever transmission was worked by two foot pedals, the left hand one changing the two forward speeds, the centre pedal selected reverse while another pedal operated the transmission brake. The tricks that could be played with the pedals were amusing, as the transmission was most forgiving. Even if a learner selected reverse while travelling at full speed it did no harm except to slow the car slightly, and indeed Ford recommended that reverse be used to slow the car occasionally to equalise wear on the drive bands. Another ingenious feature of the Model T was the generator, which was energised by flywheel-mounted magnets which revolved close to a ring carrying 16 coils. The current was fed to the distributor, then to the four trembler coils and finally to the spark plugs. A battery was fitted and by 1915 electric lights and a hooter were standard equipment.

The sketchy four-seater body looked very spindly set up on top of the chassis, which itself perched above the transverse leaf spring sus-

Early and late Model T Fords – a 1909 example (*top*) and a Model T of 1925 (*centre*), just before it went out of production. Its successor was the Model A (*right*).

26

pension. The car was very light, seldom weighing more than 1700 lb even with the windscreen, rudimentary hood and one or two other creature comforts.

Many legends grew up round the Model T, not the least being Henry Ford's alleged remark about being able to buy one in any colour as long as it was black. On a more serious note, one or two historians have stated that the Model T probably had greater effect on the development of America than any other single factor; it certainly played a bigger part in opening up the West than its horse-drawn predecessors.

Regarded early on as something of a joke (and smashed to pieces in numerous Keystone Cops films) the legendary reliability of the Model T soon spread far and wide; as long as there was some oil in the sump and a drop of petrol in the tank it would run, even when the moving parts had worn considerably. It was often a poor starter in cold weather and when the transmission bands wore it did not like climbing hills, but the driver simply reversed uphill! The flood of Model Ts became a torrent, so that Ford was able to reduce the price from 850 dollars in 1908 when it was announced, to 490 dollars in 1914, and even after the war in 1919 it cost only 525 dollars, which was about £130.

Assembly plants for the car were set up in many countries, including England, where before the First World War pilot production was started at Trafford Park in Manchester. The price was little more than £140. After the war the Model T became very popular in England, despite its engine which was a lot larger than economics dictated. The car's low purchase price and reliability made up for its low top speed and higher than average fuel consumption (it would rarely exceed 40 mph and was capable of 25 mpg).

The Model T boom lasted until 1923, but while Ford concentrated on the production of one model the rest of the industry had worked hard to recoup their positions in the face of Ford's tremendous success, which had given the Model T over two-thirds of the American market. Other makes such as Chevrolet began to make inroads into the Ford market,

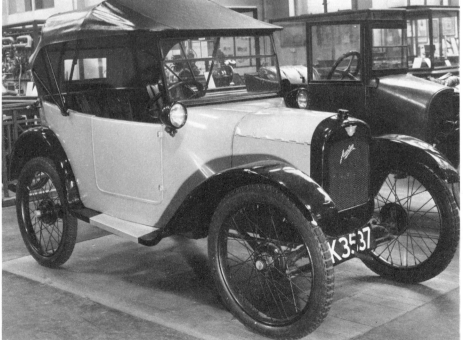

Top: a 1913 example of the marque Chevrolet, which was to tumble Ford from supremacy. The Austin 7 – this is a 1922 tourer (*left*) – was a British equivalent of the T.

Opposite, top: the 10·8 hp Clyno of
1927. This marque, and many others,
succumbed in the face of mass
production methods of Morris and
Austin. The 1924 Delage DI 14/40
(*left*) was the mainstay of Delage
production in the early 1920s.
Above: the Italian Lancia Lambda
was a revolutionary design,
pioneering monocoque construction. It had an overhead camshaft
V4 engine, and a vertical coil
spring independent front suspension which was used by Lancia
until the 1960s. The Lambda was in
production from 1922 until 1931.

but the rear axle was suspended on quarter elliptic leaf springs. The 698 cc engine gave a modest 10 bhp but since the tiny car with its wheelbase of 6 ft 6 in. weighed little more than 780 lb, it could reach a precarious top speed of 40 mph. Four-wheel brakes were standard, although the foot brake acted only on the rear wheels. The hand brake worked on the front wheels.

Success was almost immediate for the Austin Seven and it was soon selling at the rate of 200 a week at a price of £165. Improvements were made during its life, such as an increase in capacity to 747 cc in 1924, and synchromesh was introduced in the late 1920s on all but first gear. A three-bearing crankshaft replaced the spidery two-bearing arrangement and the brakes were also improved. All sorts of sports bodies were built for construction on the simple A-shape Austin Seven chassis, and just as with the Model T the engine was often highly tuned for racing. Even today the 750 Motor Club still uses Austin Seven based units for racing and trials, some 50 years after the model was first announced. Thousands of Sevens were exported and built under licence; the Seven was known as the Rosengart in France, the Dixi in Germany and the Bantam in America, where it had more novelty value than anything else. The price of the Seven gradually dropped during its life, reaching a low of £115 in the Depression.

The Austin Seven and the flat-twin air-cooled Rover Eight which preceded it by a couple of years were serious opposition to the cyclecar and William Morris soon applied the *coupe de grace* to a number of small manufacturers with his Morris Cowley and Minor models. Morris had started building cars in 1912, but they achieved little prominence until the 1920s. His cars had been reasonably expensive but, hit by money troubles in 1922 he started cutting his prices drastically, which had the effect of immediately boosting sales. This allowed Morris to pay off his debts, expand and even take in other companies such as Hotchkiss, who supplied his engines, Léon Bollée in France and Wolseley and S.U. in England. The 'Bullnose' Morris Cowley began to sell in large numbers, although its specification was pretty conventional and its four-cylinder engine twice the size of the Austin Seven's. However, prices began to drop near to the level of that of the

and eventually Henry Ford was obliged to introduce a new car, the Model A, which appeared in the autumn of 1927. The A was a fairly ordinary car which never sold as well as the T, and Ford never again dominated the market. But that 18-year production run produced nearly 15 million Model Ts, a record that was to stand until 1972 when Volkswagen's Beetle finally usurped it, in very different conditions.

The Model T had set many other car manufacturers thinking and in 1922 Sir Herbert Austin, who had

Top: **William Morris in one of his Bullnose cars. The Morris factory in pre-production line days (*above*).**

previously made worthy, though unexciting, medium and large sized cars, announced the Austin Seven. This tiny machine could well be likened to the Model T in its conception as well as its execution, for it featured a four-cylinder side-valve engine with a detachable head, in unit with the three-speed gearbox. Front suspension was by a similar transverse leaf spring set-up to that in the Model T,

A 1927 Singer Junior on its way to Monte Carlo, when just to arrive in the famous Rally was a feat.

Austin Seven and over 2,000 a week were being turned out in 1927, by which time the shapely 'Bullnose' had given way to a flat radiator.

In 1928 Morris, now Sir William, decided to produce a vehicle in direct competition with the Austin and introduced the overhead camshaft 847 cc four-cylinder Morris Minor. This little car was capable of 55 mph and in tourer form sold for a competitive £125. The half elliptic suspension and four-wheel brakes were considered to be much better than those of the Austin Seven and soon over 100 cars a day were being produced. Later, Morris was to reduce the price to £100 when the car failed to achieve dominance over Austin.

In America, the Budd Manufacturing Company developed a process of welding bodies from steel panels, thus eliminating the tiresome and expensive hand building which had previously been necessary. Dodge cars went over to this process in 1923 and William Morris was quick to realise its possibilities. By 1927, Morris was converting his factory to the Budd system. This method of construction was used on the 1935 Morris Eight, which finally gave Morris sales dominance over Austin. The fully equipped and modern looking saloon sold at £132. By 1939, the Morris organisation included Riley, while MG had been under their wing for many years.

Austin and Morris dominated the small and inexpensive car market in the 1920s and 1930s, to the extent firms such as Clyno, Trojan, Lea-Francis, Swift, Calthorpe, Arrol-Johnston and Gwynne were forced

Above: a tourer version of the famous Bullnose Morris, so named because of the shape of its radiator.
Opposite, top: one of the first Citroens, the Type A 1·3 litre model of 1919 which sold in large numbers.
Right: the 7CV Citroen of 1934 which introduced front wheel drive to the masses. This classic car stayed in production until 1957.

out of business. In the 1930s, however, the Ford factory at Dagenham on the Thames Estuary began to build the Model Y and later the Eight, which sold at £100 and gave Austin and Morris a great deal of competition.

In France, Citroen was dominant in the manufacture of cars for the masses, closely followed by Renault. The 1921 5CV 'Cloverleaf' Citroen set the standard and pace for baby cars and later Citroen led the way again by being the first European manufacturer to use the Budd all-steel body construction method. In French markets the 6CV Renault gave Citroen serious sales competition while Peugeot's 5CV Quadrilette was hovering on the verge of mass production. In Germany only Opel made any impression on the mass market between the two wars, mainly due to Germany's depressed economy, but before the Second World War, the seeds of a motoring revolution that was later to impress the world were sown by Hitler in his support for the Volkswagen — the people's car.

In Italy, only Fiat really catered for the mass market, although a number of technically advanced and sporting machines were being built by other manufacturers.

The Second World War heralded the way for the true mass market. Before it, a car that sold a million was a sensation, but if a popular small car in the 1970s does not sell a million in five years it is a comparative failure.

FORLORN HOPES

The history of the automobile is dotted with innumerable ill-conceived and mis-planned ideas and schemes which reached the production stage, but at each end of the spectrum were too advanced or ridiculous to succeed, while a number of worthy designs failed, usually for lack of money. Even established manufacturers have occasionally made mistakes and have paid dearly for their miscalculations.

One of the biggest failures from an established manufacturer was the Chrysler Airflow of 1934. Chrysler came into existence in 1923 and rapidly became one of America's major manufacturers, taking over

curved screen, concealed luggage boot, rear-wheel spats and full width grille did not appeal to American tastes and the model lost Chrysler a lot of money. Also it was not a very good car to drive, since to enable the passenger space to fit within the wheelbase the straight eight engine was hung over the front axle, making the ride rather bouncy on poor roads. The model lasted until 1937, in modified form, then was

range, but instead of designing a new up-market Ford or a down-market Mercury, they decided to announce a new marque, naming it Edsel, which was the christian name of one of Henry Ford's sons. Technically the cars were much the same as Ford and Mercury models with 5·9 litre and 6·7 litre V8 engines with a choice of push button automatic or manual transmission. Bodily, the car was very much in the current American

Maxwell and Dodge, and then launching Plymouth and de Soto. Their cars were fairly adventurous in design by contemporary American standards, but the Airflow was just too advanced for the American buyers of the times. The technical specification was not revolutionary, but the body styling broke away from the traditional upright stance of American saloons. The flowing aerodynamic shape of the Airflow with headlights flush with the front wings,

quietly dropped. Since that day Chrysler have not been noted for great technical ingenuity or leadership in styling advances, and it can be of little consolation that many aspects of the Airflow were later copied with success by other manufacturers.

The Airflow was not the only disaster by an American manufacturer, for Ford perpetrated an even worse misjudgement in 1957. They decided that there was a gap between the Ford models at the lower end of their price range and the mid-market Mercury

style except for a huge vertical front grille, which was as out of vogue as the Airflow had been 23 years earlier. Virtually all American cars of 1957 had vast wide horizontal grilles and it seems probable that the main factor which killed the Edsel was quite simply its grille. Despite the introduction of a cheaper six-cylinder model, the Edsel marque name was dropped in 1959 after a mere two years of production.

A more tragic American failure was that of the abortive Tucker, which according to those who drove one of the few cars to be made was a promising design. Designed by Pres-

ton Tucker immediately after the Second World War, the car was far ahead of the other American designs of the period as it featured independent suspension, disc brakes and a rear-mounted flat-six Franklin engine giving 150 bhp. It was a biggish car with a 10 ft 8 in wheelbase, which weighed around 3,500 lb; a great deal of attention was paid to safety. Body styling was the work of ex-Auburn and Cord designer, Alex Tremulis, the most notable feature being the three headlamp system at the front. The car suffered from gearbox problems, as the original preselector four-speed transmission proved troublesome. Great interest was aroused by the design, with car dealers clamouring to be granted a selling franchise and Tucker was able to persuade many of them to invest in his Company, before he became involved in a law suit with the Government on a fraud charge. By the time he was acquitted all confidence in the project had been lost and it had to be abandoned after fewer than fifty cars had been built.

The most amusing and intriguing white elephants have been in the luxury car class. One of the strangest vehicles was the Bucciali, built by the two Bucciali brothers in Paris. The pair of them inherited a large fortune and they spent it by building a number of technically interesting small cars; they used front wheel drive, independent suspension by rubber, infinitely variable automatic transmission, and other novelties. But the cars sold in infinitesimal numbers and indeed the Bucciali brothers never seemed to attempt to sell their cars. Their most extravagant design was the Double-Eight of 1931 and 1932. This vast machine sported a pair of straight eight Continental engines, modified to mount side by side on a common crankcase and still retaining the separate crankshafts, which were geared together. The engines were each said to give 130 bhp from their 3·8 litres capacity. Although the huge saloon appeared at the Paris Show in successive years, it is believed that it never ran under its own power and no other example was ever built. After one or two more experiments, the Bucciali brothers stopped 'making' cars in 1933.

England was by no means devoid of eccentrics, for in 1930 Sir Dennistoun Burney, the airship designer, came up with a strange looking device called the Burney Streamline. It was an enormous 20 ft long machine designed along early aerodynamic

Opposite: the Chrysler Airflow of 1934 – a design disaster for the American firm.
Top: the controversial grille of the 1957 Edsel. The massive Bucciali Double-Eight of 1931 (*centre*), with a 260 bhp V16 engine: it never went into production. *Bottom:* the 1932 Burney Streamline sedan with Lycoming engine. It attracted wide attention, but priced at £1,500, it was a commercial failure.

principles with a straight eight 3 litre twin-cam Beverley engine mounted in the tail. With all independent suspension, a four-speed overdrive gearbox, hydraulic brakes and a capatious interior it was a quite advanced design, but it cost £1,500 in 1930 and the peculiar shape was not a saleable proposition, despite the publicity afforded when the Prince of Wales bought a Burney in 1931. The project was taken over by Crossley Motors who fitted a smaller engine and modified body to give a more conventional appearance but this effort soon petered out.

A similar fate had befallen Edmund Rumpler's Tropfenwagen saloon of the early 1920s, and his Benz Grand Prix cars of 1923. Both were rear-engined cars with streamlined bodies, in conception well ahead of their times, and within the practical knowledge then available perhaps too far

Left: the Rumpler 'Tropfenwagen' or 'teardrop' saloon, with rear mounted 2·6 litre 6 cylinder engine. Based on the Rumpler, the 1923 North-Lucas (*below*) featured a 1½ litre 5 cylinder radial engine.

Above: typical cyclecar was the American built Imp, a tandem two seater with a vee twin engine and a fearsome belt drive transmission. The 1913 Carden cyclecar (*right*) was a single seater with vee twin rear-mounted engine and rudimentary accommodation.

ahead. The radial-engined North-Lucas of 1923 was another essay on these lines, but it was largely left to the Czechoslovak Tatra firm to persevere with large rear-engined saloons, using V8 engines. Their 87 was in production from 1937 until 1941, and in 1957 the 603 with a rear-mounted V8 was introduced.

An American machine rather similar in shape to the Burney was the Dymaxion, which was designed by Buckminster Fuller in 1933. This was a three-wheeler mainly built of dural and balsa wood, with power coming from a Ford V8. It achieved 120 mph on test, which emphasised the excellent aerodynamic properties. It later crashed, killing two passengers, and only two Dymaxions were subsequently built, one of which still exists in America.

The cyclecar era in Britain produced some very rudimentary machines. Perhaps the crudest example, at least at the outset, was the AV Monocar. As the name suggests, it

Above: one of the most glorious white elephants of all time was the Type 41 Bugatti Royale. It had a 13-litre 300 horse power straight eight engine. Only seven were made, but Bugatti adapted the engine to power railcars.

Left: Wolseley made this Gyrocar for the Russian inventor Count Schilowsky.

carried only the driver who sat in a sort of boat-shaped body which came to a sharp point at the front. The V-twin motorcycle engine, usually a J.A.P. or Blackburne of around 1,100 cc, was fitted immediately behind the driver, who if incautious enough to lean back could receive an

involuntary warming up from the cylinder head or a shock from an exposed spark plug! The engine was started by a chain wound round an extension shaft on the flywheel; the driver gave the chain a hard tug, but he had to ensure that if the engine backfired he could let go of the chain quickly, or he would be wound into the machinery! Surprisingly, the AV was quite popular despite its dangerous handling characteristics, and when a more civilised two seater was devised it remained in production until 1926, by which time the Austin Seven had killed most rival cyclecars.

Another ingenious machine was the G.W.K., with a main claim to fame in its friction drive. Devised in 1910 by Messrs Grice, Wood and Keiller, the G.W.K. friction drive system used the engine flywheel as the driving disc which engaged another disc set at right angles to it. The second disc was originally faced with compressed paper, but later with cork, the idea being that the disc could be engaged at four different points to allow gear steps. Unfortunately, there was a great deal of slip on early models, necessitating frequent replacement of the friction material. Later modifications improved the car's performance but friction drive had earned a bad name and few G.W.K.s were sold once the cyclecar boom was over.

A splendidly magnificent white elephant was the Bugatti Royale, built by Ettore Bugatti, who designed so many fine sporting cars. In 1927 Bugatti decided to build a magnificent car to compete with the Rolls-Royce and Hispano-Suiza. With a wheelbase of 14 ft 2 in it was the largest car in production and was powered by a straight-eight engine of nearly 13 litres capacity (the engine alone was nearly 5 ft long). It was said to give 300 bhp at 2,000 rpm and would propel the vast machine at 125 mph. Bugatti grandly let it be known that he would build only twenty-five cars, all of which would be sold to the crowned heads of Europe — hence the name Royale. Unfortunately, there were not sufficient crowned heads, and many of those who might have been interested in the Royale could hardly spend £5,000 on one car. In the end, only seven were made, six of which exist in museums and private collections, mostly in America. Bugatti adroitly turned what might have been a huge loss into a handsome profit by selling a batch of Royale engines to the French railways for use in rail cars.

Some designers had a passion for fitting cars with more wheels than was necessary, ignoring the fact that steering may be made difficult, if not impossible. Perhaps the champion of this trend was the Reeves Company of Columbus, Indiana. Reeves started off in a conventional fashion but in 1911 they took an Overland and fitted it with an extra pair of axles, one at the front and one at the rear, somehow contriving to steer six of the wheels! Quite how this vehicle steered and handled is not clear, but presumably it caused difficulties because production of the Octuato, as it was called, was rapidly stopped and a new model with only six wheels was introduced. This one, improbably called the Sexauto, had two wheels at the front and four at the rear, but by 1913 the Company had gone out of business.

Citroen went even further in the early 1920s by building cars and commercial vehicles with a half-track system invented by Adolphe Kegresse. In this design the vehicle retained the normal steered front wheels but the rear end was fitted with a system similar to tank tracks, except that his tracks used rubber and canvas instead of metal, enabling the vehicles to be driven on roads. Kegresse adapted the normal 10 hp Citroen car and the system was arranged so that the cars could be converted from the normal four-wheel layout to half tracks in two hours by two men. Citroen built a set of vehicles using half-tracks to make the first successful car crossing of the Sahara Desert during Christmas time 1922. The team of Citroens crossed the Sahara from Touggourt to Timbuktu in 21 days. The publicity gained from this exercise gave half-track vehicles a short spell of popularity but this form of traction was needed only on rough terrain and was of real value only on military vehicles.

Perhaps the prize for the oddest car of all goes to the Wolseley Gyrocar, although maybe the credit or blame for this device should not be placed on Wolseley since they only manufactured it for its inventor, the Russian Count Schilowsky. The Gyrocar was a two wheeler fitted with a Wolseley engine which powered twin gyros as well as driving the car. The gyros adequately stabilised the machine once it was running but they used a lot of power. Because the Gyrocar could do nothing that the normal four-wheeled car could not do better, it never proceeded beyond the prototype state.

REVIVAL

At the end of the Second World War most European countries lay in ruins and of the major car industries only the American survived intact. Even in the United States, most factories had been producing war materials, so for a period until these could be converted back to peacetime production the motorist had to rely on pre-war cars. In Europe, the extreme shortage of cars, money, fuel and spares meant that few cars were on the roads, and those that were sold for astronomical prices. It was not unusual to be asked to pay £200 for a ten-year old machine which had only cost just over £100 when new. Fuel was rationed and most new cars produced were only available to buyers who could prove a genuine business need, and in Britain buyers of new cars had to sign a covenant not to sell the car within a specified period.

Of the big British manufacturers, Austin announced their post war plans in November 1944, although production did not commence until a year later, after hostilities had ended. Austin concentrated on pre-war models, the Eight, Ten and Twelve plus the Sixteen, which used a new 2·2 litre engine developed during the war. At Morris Motors, production also centred on pre-war models, the Series E Eight and Series M Ten, both of which had been developed in 1938. At the Ford Factory in Dagenham production was also recommenced with a pair of pre-war survivors, the Anglia and the Prefect, both powered by the well-known side-valve engine, which was to introduce many subsequently famous names to motor sport. Hillman began building the Minx, which was virtually the same as the pre-war model. The Standard company commenced

Above: **a 1946 Standard Flying Fourteen saloon, a typical carry-on from pre-war production.** *Opposite:* **this vast and vulgar Buick of 1949 contrasts with the simplicity of the Morris Minor of 1948.**

with the Eight and Ten, and Wolseley with the 8, 10, 12, 14 and 18 — all based on pre-war models. Only Riley introduced new models, the 1½ and 2½ litre. The 2½ litre had the dubious distinction of having the longest stroke engine in current production, at 120 mm — a legacy of the RAC horsepower tax which based the road tax on the cylinder bore of an engine.

Of the specialist makers, Jaguar recommenced production with 1½, 2½ and 3½ litre saloons. Triumph began with 1800 saloons and roadsters and MG introduced the immortal TC, which resembled the pre-war TB in most details.

On the Continent, where many factories had been reduced to rubble, production restarted even more slowly, few firms being in serious production until 1946. The German industry was not allowed to resume manufacture until given permission by the Allies, and so its return was prolonged even further. Japan hardly had a motor industry before the war and

so was not taken into account. Only in America was a smooth return to peacetime motoring possible, for no concessions had to be made to economy as fuel was in plentiful supply and some factories had been producing cars throughout the war. In a desperate bid for release from wartime restrictions American cars became vast and vulgar and for the first time 'styling', as distinct from aesthetic design, was considered. The decade of the huge chrome fender, dummy porthole, and tail fins arrived, and was aped in Europe.

But within two or three years from the end of the war the world's motor industries began to prepare for the predicted export bonanza. British

manufacturers were so busy coping with orders that many of them neglected further development, continuing to build slightly modernised versions of pre-war models. However, on the Continent a revolution was in progress which was soon to sweep Britain from its position as second largest automobile manufacturer. Many of the French, German and Italian car builders saw that the depressed economy of the post-war years called for small, reliable, economical cars which were cheap to service and easy to maintain. They opted for the rear-engined configuration and soon the world's markets were swarming with Volkswagens, Fiats and Renaults.

British manufacturers were slow to react to this trend and few of them bothered to heed the warning signs. Ingenuity was not dead but it was often stifled. Austin vigorously encouraged the sales of such vehicles as the Austin Atlantic and A40 sports in North America, but once their novelty value had worn off and poor reliability was revealed sales dropped off dramatically. Alec Issigonis developed the first significant new postwar British car when he designed the Morris Minor for the Nuffield organisation in 1948. With an ingenious torsion bar front suspension (adopted over 20 years later on the Morris Marina) and a rigid rear axle on leaf springs the new car handled like a sports car, and it revolutionised the stagnant British industry. The body looks bulbously outdated today but in 1948 the all-steel monocoque body and chassis unit, which was one of the first unit construction chassis, was very advanced. Unfortunately, Issigonis was not given his head in all aspects of the design — he wanted to use a flat twin air-cooled engine together with a new all-synchromesh gearbox but he was obliged to use the pre-war Series E side-valve engine and gearbox. Despite this handicap the Minor soon became the best selling British car, appearing in almost every possible guise, including two- and four-door saloons, a convertible and the famous wood-framed estate car, as well as a van and pick-up truck. Performance was improved in 1952 by the use of an 803 cc overhead-valve engine, which was later increased to 948 cc and subsequently 1098 cc. Several attempts were made by other manufacturers to usurp the Minor's position but steady demand kept it on the production lines for over 20 years, during which time its sales soared way over a million.

While the British were applauding

the Minor, an even greater revolution was fermenting in Germany, one which was to sweep most other foreign makes off the American market and cause even the American giants such as General Motors, Chrysler and Ford to change their tactics. The idea of the Volkswagen (people's car) was conceived in a rare moment of perspicacity by Adolf Hitler, who decided that his people needed a basic and extremely cheap car. Dr Ferdinand Porsche the noted racing car designer, won the commission to design the car and although Porsche was unable to get anywhere near the low price of 990 Reichsmarks demanded by Hitler, he did evolve a revolutionary small car based on designs which he had already been working on for several years. With a flat platform mated to a central backbone chassis an air-cooled flat-four engine in the tail and full independent suspension, the Volkswagen was in advance of its time. It barely got into production before the Second World War, but the various scout car and other military versions produced during the war, all helped the development of the basic car. After the war, an Allied investigation team turned down the opportunity of building the Volkswagen and eventually its production was resumed in Germany. The success of the VW is now history, for in 1972 the Volkswagen 'Beetle' surpassed the Model T Ford as the biggest selling car ever made; planes, as well as providing a basis for the famous range of Porsche sports cars. When Germany was allowed to export cars in the early 1950s, the Beetle soon flooded the American market and gradually infiltrated other areas until it rapidly became the top selling import in many countries.

America had been wedded to the idea of big cars for many years but the popularity of tiny imported cars such as the VW, following on the success of sports cars from Jaguar, MG, Triumph and Austin-Healey, made the car industry moguls hesitate, and in the 1950s Ford and Chrysler announced 'compact' cars, the Ford Falcon and Chrysler Valiant. However, they were compact only to American eyes, still being large by

Opposite: a row of Volkswagen prototypes during early testing in 1937. The lack of rear windows seems to be taking cost cutting, to meet Hitler's selling price requirements, too far. Some 35 years later the VW shape is still apparent in this 1973 model 1303 (*left*).
Above: one of the world's finest line of sports cars, the Porsche, was developed from the humble VW. This is the 1948 prototype.

although sales started decreasing in the 1970s, they remained enormous.

The bulbous Beetle had many faults, such as lack of interior room, little luggage space, poor handling characteristics from its swing axle rear suspension and instability in side winds, but it had the one great virtue of consumate reliability. The British VW importers began giving certificates to people who had achieved 65,000 miles on the same engine but so many were claimed that the project had to be abandoned — the cars just kept going for ever. The basic engine size was increased from 1131 cc to 1600 cc, and the reliable, slow revving unit has been seen in everything from racing cars to aero-

European standards, and the six-cylinder cars never looked like impinging on the 10 per cent of total car sales in America achieved by imported cars. Soon both the Falcon and Valiant were available with large V8 engines and for a while the industry turned its back on the attempts to build 'small' cars.

Chevrolet attempted to compete with the Volkswagen by building a 'bigger Volkswagen', the Corvair. This vehicle had a flat-six, air-cooled engine in the tail and a similar swing axle rear suspension to that of the VW. It was a much larger car than the Beetle and although moderately popular for a while it could make no impression on VW sales. In an attempt

The utility Citroen 2CV, the car which mobilised rural France. This version, the Sahara, was for cross country work.

to push sales, the Corvair was given a sporty image with coupe and convertible versions, but the Corvair production ceased when Ralph Nader, the American car safety campaigner, flourished evidence about the allegedly dangerous handling characteristics of the rear suspension, and a number of owners who had suffered crashes sued General Motors for damages. However, Chevrolet did have a success when they developed the glass fibre bodied Corvette sports car. This car competed well with imported cars and although sales were minimal by American standards (25,000 a year) it filled a gap, and in its Sting Ray form it sold well.

On the Continent, French and Italian manufacturers were competing directly with the Volkswagen. In France, the 'Quatre Chevaux' Renault and 'Deux Chevaux' Citroen were doing sterling service as basic transport, the versatile little Citroen being particularly popular with the farming community. The front engine, front-wheel drive Citroen was followed by larger versions, such as the Dyane and Ami models, which retained the

same basic characteristics. The Dauphine replaced the 4CV in the Renault range. In Italy the tiny twin-cylinder, air-cooled, rear-engined Fiat 500, successor to the pre-war Topolino, was beginning to rescue many people from a life spent on Lambretta and Vespa scooters and the bigger four-cylinder, water-cooled 600 model supplemented it later on. All these cars were capable of top speeds in the 60 to 70 mph range and it was possible to achieve a fuel consumption of 40 mpg, which was exactly what was needed in the 1950s when most economies were still recovering from the war.

For people who could not afford the cheap cars of the day the bubble car flourished briefly, just as the cyclecar did after the First World War. Many of these bubble cars were designed in Germany where Heinkel, Goggomobil and Messerschmitt were best known. Their tiny air-cooled motorcycle engines endowed them with a surprising turn of speed (a party trick of the Messerschmitt was that it had four reverse gears as well as four forward gears — the direction of

rotation of the engine was altered when reversing was necessary).

Owing to a peculiarity of British law which allowed holders of motorcycle licences to drive cars which had three wheels and no reverse gear, the three-wheeler lived on in Britain long after they were abandoned in other countries (save for special purposes, such as the utility vehicles based on the scooters in Italy). Among British manufacturers were the Bond Minicar, the Scootacar, Reliant, Noble, Berkeley and Meadows Frisky. Out of all the firms which made three wheelers in the 1950s only Reliant remained in business into the 1970s, when increasing prosperity made the three wheeler a rather spartan eccentricity.

In Japan, little publicity was given to the gradual build up of a motor industry. Nissan were building the Austin A40 under licence in the 1950s, Isuzu began making the Hillman Minx and Hino built the Renault

4CV. The Japanese were busily supplying their own market in the immediate post-war period and the West was little aware of the developments which were to come. But by the late 1960s the Japanese were building more cars than the British, whose cars they had been building under licence only ten years earlier.

British manufacturers of popular cars did not keep pace with their European counterparts, usually preferring to build conventional water-cooled, front-engined cars with rigid rear axles on semi-elliptic leaf springs. These cars were unsuitable for the bumpy roads in many parts of the

The Fiat Topolino, which was built from 1936 until 1948, when it was superseded by the Fiat 500.

Continent and the British share of the European market diminished while the American small car market was dominated by the Germans with the VW. This mattered little in the early 1950s, as the home market absorbed every car made but the tide was turning before the end of the decade.

Many manufacturers had fallen into financial trouble and such well-known names as Armstrong Siddeley, Lea-Francis, and Alvis slipped quietly into oblivion while less prominent firms such as Allard, Frazer-Nash, H.R.G., Invicta, and Sunbeam-Talbot also ceased business. A series of almost inevitable company mergers began to change the face of the industry, the biggest coming in 1952 when Austin merged with Nuffield, which previously had gathered in Riley, Wolseley, and MG to add to Morris.

The resultant British Motor Corporation became Britain's largest motor company. Standard and Triumph had merged immediately after the war, then the Rootes group was formed with Hillman, Humber, Singer, Sunbeam, and Commer under its wing. Only Ford and Vauxhall of the former big five motor manufacturers continued virtually unchanged, but Vauxhall was already a fully owned subsidiary of America's General Motors and Ford during the 1950s became a wholly owned branch of American Ford. The trend was not confined to Britain. In Germany, Borgward and Glas succumbed to financial problems, in Italy Alfa Romeo became a state owned company and in America the respected Studebaker company finally ceased business after a long, agonising and

MG. Cecil Kimber in MG number one (*above*). The K3 MG Magnette (*right*) was one of the best known and most successful racing MGs. *Opposite:* the MG TC, the car which the Americans 'discovered' just after the second world war (*top*). The latest MGB which is available as a convertible and a GT coupé (*bottom*).

protracted death, which was not alleviated by the introduction of a pseudo sports saloon, the Avanti. These were only the first of many such mergers and liquidations.

There were several bright spots in the mass of mediocrity which was emanating from British factories, for British quality cars were still highly respected and popular sports cars were in great demand everywhere. The MG TC started the boom in the early 1950s when many young Americans, looking for an outlet after the frustrating years of war, turned to the sports car. The TC was followed by the TD, TF and then the first of the all-enveloping bodied MGs, the MGA which was announced in 1955. In the same year the Triumph TR2 was unveiled while the Austin-Healey 100, designed by Donald Healey and produced by Austin, had come on to the scene in 1952. These three makes took a major share of the American sports car market. The demand from the USA was so great that over 80 per cent of production was reserved for

the States. Continental manufacturers made little attempt to compete in this market and any open cars they did make were usually of the sports/tourer variety, and not 'real' sports cars.

Further up the price scale was the Jaguar XK120, a car which was a sensation when it was announced in 1948. Its sleek, flowing lines and powerful twin-overhead camshaft engine was a revelation for the day and even though production did not commence until 1950, the car was still way ahead of the opposition. It was followed by the XK140 and 150, neither of which were quite as popular. At the same time, the Jaguar saloons such as Mk VII, VIII, IX and X were among the few British saloons to sell well in the States.

British quality cars continued to do well during the 1950s, although several Continental manufacturers such as Mercedes-Benz began to challenge in export markets. The Rolls-Royce was still considered the best car in the world, and sold to the rich or discriminating as fast as they could be made, as did the Bentley. Other quality marques such as Bristol, AC, Aston Martin, Jensen, Daimler, Alvis and Lagonda all had their

Jaguar. Early cars, such as the Swallow-bodied Austin 7 and the 1935 SS Airline (*opposite*), based on a Standard chassis and engine, used proprietary components.
Top: the 1953 Le Mans winning C-type Jaguar with Duncan Hamilton driving and Tony Rolt beside him, and (*left*) the classic road-going XK120. 3·8 litre saloons in action at Brands Hatch in 1962 (*below*).

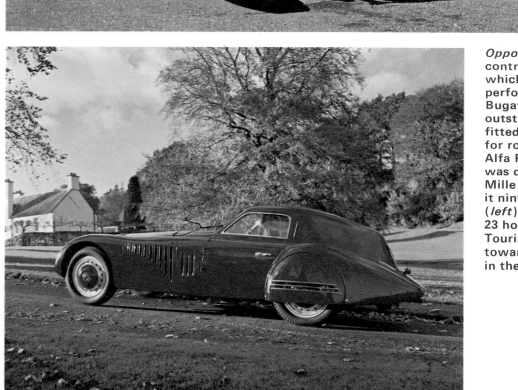

Opposite: American and European contrasts: the Auburn Speedster, which had a guaranteed 100 mph performance, and the classic Bugatti Type 35B, which had an outstanding racing record, and was fitted with cycle wings and lights for road use.

Alfa Romeos. This 1931 2·3 litre 8C was driven by Tazio Nuvolari in the Mille Milglia that year. He placed it ninth. The 2·9 litre Alfa Romeo (*left*) led the 1939 Le Mans race for 23 hours. The body by Superleggera Touring is an example of the trend towards aerodynamics which grew in the late 1930s.

Above: the Cunningham C3 coupé with Chrysler V8 engine was Briggs Cunningham's attempt to enter the GT market. It is remarkably similar in style to the 407 Bristol (*left*) which was also powered by a Chrysler V8.
Opposite: the Mini revolution-ised British motoring in 1959 and also gained numerous racing and rallying successes. The Ford Anglia 105E was Ford's conventional answer to the Mini.

adherents, but the financial difficulties facing specialist manufacturers were enormous, and many were not to survive.

The traditional car building countries, England, France, Germany Italy and the USA were gradually joined by other nations anxious to establish an industry. Sweden offered Volvo and Saab, Holland's DAF truck manufacturing company brought out a small car, India began building Austins under the name of Hindustan, Czechoslovakia's Skoda and Tatra factories began to expand, Austria began to build a variant of the Fiat 500 called the Steyr-Puch, Poland began making economy cars, Russia expanded her hitherto limited and stodgy range, Turkey began building British Reliant models under licence, East Germany built the Wartburg and Trabant, Spain established a motor industry, South American countries established factories to build American and European cars and in Australia, British, American and Japanese firms developed an expanding motor industry. In many other countries the big manufacturers set up subsidiary factories for assembling cars from parts supplied in component form.

At the end of the 1950s, British manufacturers made a determined effort to win a larger share of the market. The renaissance was led, not unexpectedly, by the man who had given the industry a shot in the arm eleven years earlier — Alec Issigonis when he designed the Mini. This burst on a startled world in 1959; although neither front-wheel drive nor a transverse engine layout were entirely original the combination in the little Mini, together with its unique rubber cone suspension, tiny 10 inch wheels and commodious interior appeared to be unbeatable. Again Issigonis wanted to use a new engine but in the interests of economy the venerable A series had to be used, modified to incorporate the gearbox into its sump. It promised to be a world beater, but initially was not as successful as it might have been because its development time was too short. Serious problems dogged it for several years, costing BMC a great deal of money in warranty claims. Nevertheless, most of the problems were overcome, and eventually the Mini became the largest selling British car ever made, although it never looked like approaching the VW Beetle's sales figures and was not a universal export success.

Ford opted for a more conventional approach to the 1960s with their Anglia, the only unconventional aspect of which was its reverse angle rear window. However its tough little overhead valve engine became one of the most popular power units of all time, powering many racing and rally cars to success.

The 1950s ran out with the rear-engined cars still on the crest of a wave, but the Mini was pointing the way to the next major development— although few but the most perceptive realised what was to come.

Left: a pre-war classic is the 1938 V12 Lagonda Rapide. It was fitted with a 4·4 litre single overhead camshaft V12 engine which gave 175 bhp at 5500 rpm.
Below: the 1953 R-type Continental Bentley is one of the most sought after post-war cars. Its 4·9 litre engine was capable of propelling it at speeds in excess of 120 mph.

THE SIXTIES AND SEVENTIES

The end of the 1950s conveniently marked a turning point in the story of motoring, for the rear-engine revolution began to wane as the industry turned to front-wheel drive. This was of course by no means a novelty — the American designer Walter Christie had built front-wheel drive cars with transverse engines in the period between 1904 and 1910. The staunchest proponents of front-wheel drive, Citroen, had built front-wheel drive cars since the 1930s, and indeed since the end of the Second World War have built nothing else, while the Swedish company Saab started car production with the front wheel drive Model 92 in 1950. However, few manufacturers in the mass market had bothered with front-wheel drive because they felt the expense was not justified on cheap cars. The Mini changed their minds — it showed just how much room could be made available in a very small package by putting the majority of the mechanical components at the front. The Mini abounded with door pockets, parcel shelves, even space under the rear seat, as well as a reasonable sized boot. Apart from Citroen's 2CV the Mini dominated the front-wheel drive market for a year or two, then Peugeot brought out their 204 front-wheel drive car, Renault announced the utility R4, Lancia brought out the Flavia saloon, Audi developed a range of medium sized front-wheel drive saloons and soon the trickle became a flood.

The Austin 1100, and later 1300, was added to the Mini in the BMC range, with the revolutionary water-filled hydrolastic interconnected suspension system taking the world by surprise. Renault committed themselves to a policy of front-wheel

Opposite: the ID/DS Citroen range with hydro pneumatic suspension was one of the most advanced in the world during two decades in production. *Top:* the two stroke Saab won many rallies in the 1960s. The Austin/Morris 1100/1300 (*right*) is a development of the Mini.

drive for all models and they gradually replaced their rear-engined small cars and rear-wheel drive large cars with front-wheel drive cars, the R6, R12 and R16. Peugeot too, converted their entire range to front-wheel drive, adding the 304 and 504 to the existing 204. Simca added the front-wheel drive 1100 to their range, the Lancia Fulvia joined the Flavia, and the revolutionary Wankel powered NSU Ro80 utilised front-wheel drive.

Of the large European manufacturers of mass produced cars only Ford, Volkswagen and Fiat were not

The Japanese Toyo Kogyo firm
makes more cars powered by the
Wankel rotary engine than any
other. This Mazda RX2 (*above*) is
powered by a twin rotor Wankel.
The German Mercedes Benz
company are experimenting with
the rotary engines and the CIII
coupé (*right*) is fitted with a four-
rotor Wankel unit giving 350 bhp,
endowing the car with a top speed
of 150 mph.

manufacturing front-wheel drive cars at the end of the 1960s, Fiat and Volkswagen concentrating on rear-engined cars and Ford on conventional rear-wheel drive machines. Then in 1969 Fiat capitulated by announcing the 128, a transverse engine front-wheel drive car very much in the Mini and 1100 style. They followed this with the smaller 127 to replace the 600 and 850 rear-engined cars. Volkswagen have remained faithful to the rear-engine concept, as epitomised in the Beetle, but declining sales, especially in the United States, where their rear-engined cars came under fire from Ralph Nader's safety campaign prompted VW to investigate front-

wheel drive. In 1970 the company announced the front-wheel drive K70, but this was an NSU design which VW took over when acquiring NSU, for at that time, Volkswagen's own small front-wheel drive model was only in the design stage.

This leaves only Ford and subsidiaries of American companies like Opel, Vauxhall and Chrysler (UK) who have not brought out front-wheel drive cars. Before Chrysler bought control of the British Rootes Group, the Group announced the Hillman Imp in 1963, which was probably the last all-new rear-engined car to appear for many years. This interesting car is powered by a light alloy four-cylinder engine derived from the Coventry Climax racing unit;

a punchy 875 cc overhead camshaft engine, it gave the Imp a top speed of 80 mph and fuel consumption in the region of 40 mpg. Despite its advanced specification it has never sold as well as the Mini in Great Britain.

Many experts were of the opinion that the characteristics of front-wheel drive made it difficult to utilise an engine of much more than 2 litres without causing problems with handling and steering, but in America the Oldsmobile division of General Motors completely confounded this theory with the Toronado, a large two-door model powered by a 7½ litre V8 engine, driving the front wheels through a three speed automatic transmission. This powerful 110 mph car showed

than the Oldsmobile, an 8·2 litre V8 giving a power output of 400 bhp and a top speed of 120 mph. The trend has not spread any further in the USA because motoring conditions are so different from those in Europe, where the front-wheel drive package is so appealing.

In Japan, the 1960s was a decade of incredible boom in all industries. Japanese cameras, radios, TV sets, textiles and automobiles began to pour on to world markets in ever increasing numbers. Japan's first export attacks in the motoring field were made in Australia and the USA, the result being almost instant success. In Australia the locally built Holden and Ford models could successfully

drive was dominating the market in Europe the Japanese cars would have front-wheel drive. The small Japanese cars tended to be unadventurous in the 1960s, the general configuration being a front engine, rear drive with independent front suspension by wishbones and a rigid rear axle, usually with drum brakes all round. However, the Japanese learned remarkably quickly and proved that they could develop new techniques seemingly overnight. Mazda took out a licence to build Wankel rotary engines and put the engine into mass production long before anyone else — and made the rotary engine more reliable than other manufacturers.

Opposite, top: Fiat changed from rear engines and rear drive to front engine, front wheel drive in the 1970s (this is a 128 coupé).
Opposite, centre: the Oldsmobile Toronado was the largest car using front wheel drive when it was announced in 1966. The VW K70 (*left*), Volkswagen's *volte face* from rear engines and air cooling. The Datsun 240Z (*above*) is a sports coupé.

that there are no difficulties with large engined front-wheel drive cars, and that the problems of heavy steering can be overcome by using power steering. Later on the Cadillac Division of General Motors announced a front-wheel drive model based on the Toronado, the Fleetwood Eldorado. This used an even larger engine

compete in the large car class with the Japanese, but in the smaller 'popular' categories the cars from Japan came to largely dominate the market. In America the first signs of a challenge to the Volkswagen's position as a market leader became apparent when both Toyota and Datsun dramatically increased their sales, with the small Toyota Corolla and Datsun 1000 models, which sold at very competitive prices. No technique proved too difficult for the Japanese technicians, if overhead camshaft engines were wanted by customers, then overhead camshafts they got, in remarkably short time; if a five-speed gearbox was likely to be a selling point, then a five-speed gearbox would be developed in record time; if front-wheel

No market was considered too small or too difficult for the Japanese. The British domination of the sports car market in America was attacked vigorously, first with cars which were little more than sports tourers and then with very competitive machines like the Datsun 240Z, a 125 mph sports coupe which was cleverly adapted from many existing components and made available in the US at a price which made it competitive with the British MGB. Only Honda, who dominated world motorcycle markets before starting to build cars, have been relatively unsuccessful. Their little 600 saloon was just too small for the world markets and their S800 sports car with its high-revving overhead-camshaft engine

The last of generations of stark 'hairy' sports cars – the 7 litre AC Cobra which was capable of 160 mph. The cockpit of the Cobra was spartan and functional.

Opposite: Peter Morgan poses beside the Plus 8 Morgan, powered by the Rover 3½ litre engine. This Morgan is a thriving survivor of the 'traditional' sports car, which was built by many British companies for decades – if any car can be called hand-made it is the Morgan, which still uses a wood framed body.

never appealed to a large sector of export markets and it was withdrawn from many countries. The 1300 saloon with an air-cooled engine never made an impression outside Japan.

In the early 1970s the Japanese boom showed signs of reaching its peak because overproduction had started to saturate home and export markets and many countries were wary of possible market domination by Japanese goods. The USA imposed a 10 per cent surcharge on imports and brought about a devaluation of the yen, which at least brought a temporary respite.

The American motor industry had for many years been wedded to the idea of building large, comfortable cars powered by large slow revving V8 engines. These cars proved to be fast and unwieldy, yet ideally suited to American motoring conditions, where roads are wide and straight and generally limited to a speed of 60 or 70 mph. However, the onslaught of 'Nader's Raiders', as the safety campaigners became known, began to affect the thinking of industry and many companies took steps to improve their cars. Instead of making nearly all vehicles 'full size' many more intermediate sized cars and compacts began to appear again. The 'pony car' era started with the introduction of the Ford Mustang in 1964. This medium sized four-seater saloon was styled to appeal to younger drivers who wanted a sporting image and the craze soon swept through other car companies, the Chevrolet Camaro and American Motors Javelin being outstanding examples. The cars were generally safer to drive than the larger types, because they had stiffer suspension and wider tyres giving much improved roadholding, and better brakes. The handsome Javelin

was the salvation of American Motors, which as the smallest American manufacturer looked set to follow Studebaker into bankruptcy, but the Javelin brought it back into business.

Encouraged by this success American manufacturers turned to 'muscle cars', full size with bigger engines than the pony types, which generally had engines of around 5 litres. These muscle cars, such as the Dodge Charger, Ford Torino Cobra, Plymouth Road Runner and Pontiac GTO, were all available with high performance engines giving up to 425 bhp, and chassis modifications to match. Very often these machines provided the basis for cars in the NASCAR sedan racing series, which is very popular in the States.

In the early 1960s the market prospects looked excellent for the American industry, but the permanent cloud of haze hanging over Los Angeles was to set in motion a revolution which

A typical American 'muscle car', a Dodge in action at Daytona.

had world wide repercussions. It was held that this was caused by emissions from the exhausts of the millions of cars in the Los Angeles area, and although scientists established that it in fact resulted from an unfortunate set of atmospheric conditions the State of California pressed ahead with legislation to limit the amounts of carbon monoxide and unburnt hydrocarbons released into the atmosphere through car exhausts. This had nationwide effects, for it soon became mandatory throughout the entire country. Soon, ecology became a favourite talking point for politicians and a race was on to introduce more vote catching legislation. Safety in automobiles

The NSU Ro80 with double rotor Wankel engine suffered many teething troubles.

A product of American racing, a Ford Torino Cobra at Daytona.

was the next aspect to interest the law makers and regulations were drafted to make cars safe in accidents, although the vast numbers of deaths on American roads could have been reduced considerably if full harness safety belts had been made mandatory, or if some effort had been directed to improve the handling and braking qualities of many American cars. Instead American car makers were constrained to develop expensive passive restraints, such as inflating air bags, which are likely to add £100 to the cost of a car. Restrictions are becoming tougher every year and by 1972 many American firms were stating that they cannot meet the planned

The Triumph TR series of traditional sports cars have proved very popular; this is a TR5.

pollution and safety regulations.

The result of this legislation has been to reduce the power output of the large American V8 engines which need air pumps, catalytic exhaust afterburners and other devices to meet the regulations. There are well-grounded fears that it will not be possible to meet future regulations with existing internal combustion engines and many manufacturers are already developing alternative power plants. The steam engine has many supporters and several large companies, including British Leyland and Chrysler, are investigating this form of power, although few people expect a steam unit to appear in production. American businessman Bill Lear spent a fortune on developing an automobile steam engine but was forced to admit defeat, although he has since developed a larger unit for use in trucks and buses. The gas turbine engine achieved a brief vogue in the

1950s when Chrysler, Fiat, Renault and Rover developed prototype small-car units, but although turbine engines have been used in trucks the emission problem is still present.

The Wankel rotary engine seems to be the most promising type of power unit to develop and many companies are exploring the potential of rotary engines with this factor uppermost in their engineers' minds. It has many attractions, for there are few moving parts and it is relatively simple to produce. Its main problem has been in effecting a long lasting seal to the rotor tips. The NSU Ro80 suffered numerous teething troubles because of this difficulty and many owners have been obliged to change three or four engines due to failure of the rotor seals. However, Mazda in Japan claim to have overcome this problem.

In America, General Motors have extensively developed the Wankel engine, it is believed with the intention that by 1976 they could replace their piston engines with rotary units throughout their entire range. In Germany, Mercedes-Benz are working on advanced three- and four-rotor Wankel engines, Rolls-Royce of England have developed a diesel version. Curtis-Wright in America are looking into the possibilities of very large Wankel units, and many other car builders have taken out licences to experiment with rotary engines.

The need to implement the statutary anti-pollution and new safety measures were felt throughout the world, and some manufacturers were forced to withdraw either temporarily or permanently from the lucrative American market (originally, manufacturers producing fewer than 500 cars a year were exempt from the regulations, but all cars must now comply, and many of the small firms have also been forced to withdraw from the American market). The end result may well be safer, pollution free cars, in which case the politicians will have been vindicated, but many people in the industry wish the problem had been tackled in a more realistic manner.

Many motoring enthusiasts are of the opinion that motoring for sheer pleasured died in the 1950s — in fact, many go so far as to state that real motoring ended in the 1930s, when a driver could jump into his car and drive as far and as fast as he liked without hindrance. Nowadays, the high density of traffic on the roads, speed limits, breathalyser laws, parking restrictions, high fuel costs, heavy insurance and annual car testing have a depressive effect on the driver who is forced to conform to a pattern if he is not to violate the law. This is undeniably a good thing in some ways, but many people view the motor car as the sole remaining method through which a man can show individuality and express himself.

The end of restrictions is by no means in sight, for many traffic engineers are of the opinion that forms of road pricing are inevitable. In this system, drivers will be required to pay for travelling on certain busy roads, mainly those in the centre of large towns — the nearer the centre the more expensive will motoring become. Some experts also believe that if the car population continues to rise it will be necessary to institute a form of booking system for certain busy roads, for example to coastal resorts on summer weekends; drivers will have to apply in advance for tickets to drive to a particular town or use a certain road and once the allocation of tickets is sold no one else will be allowed to use the road or visit the town.

The 1960s saw a further contraction of the world's motor industry, for a number of firms went out of business or were absorbed by larger organisations. The biggest merger and takeover battle of the decade was that which saw the formation of the British Leyland Motor Corporation in 1967. This was the cumulative result of a series of mergers and takeovers which virtually grouped the whole of the British owned motor industry under one name. The British Motor Corporation was not in a healthy position when Sir Donald Stokes, head of the Leyland-Triumph organisation, suggested a merger and when it did take place there was no doubt which

Top: the Mk. 3 Ford Cortina exemplifies a Ford trend towards extrovert styling, retaining conventional engineering.

One of the new breed of American 'compacts' is the Ford Pinto (*above*) powered by the engine used in some European Fords.

Top: an example of international cooperation is the Saab 99, powered by the Triumph-designed engine, which is built in Sweden.

Japanese contender for world markets is the front wheel drive Datsun Cherry (*above*), available in saloon and estate car forms.

was the dominant partner, for the new company name favoured Leyland and Sir Donald Stokes became Chief Executive. Leyland is a successful truck manufacturing company which had already taken over the ailing Standard-Triumph organisation. This was an end of one set of mergers as B.M.C. and Jaguar had already merged to form British Motor Holdings (Jaguar had taken over Daimler and the Coventry-Climax engine company as well as Guy trucks). BLMC made an offer to Rover in 1967 which was accepted, so Rover, who had previously acquired Alvis, joined the Corporation. This meant that one company was building models carrying the names Austin, Daimler, Jaguar, MG, Morris, Riley, Rover, Triumph, Vanden Plas and Wolseley, as well as numerous truck makes. In a policy of rationalisation, the name of Riley was soon eliminated, to be added to Standard and Alvis which had already ceased to exist, while Wolseley and Vanden Plas lasted into the 1970s only as badge-engineering names. The new company went through a very troubled period for the first two years of its life but staged a recovery to make a handsome profit in 1971.

Chrysler of America consolidated its European position by acquiring both Simca and Matra to add to the erstwhile Rootes Group. On the Continent Fiat acquired Lancia, Ferrari and Abarth, leaving only Alfa Romeo and a few smaller Italian firms out of their net, while in Germany Volkswagen bought the NSU and Audi combine. In France, Citroen took a controlling interest in the Italian Maserati concern but ran into financial problems themselves and were bailed out by Fiat who took a 49 per cent interest. Since Citroen had previously formed a holding company with NSU to build Wankel rotary powered cars, both Fiat and Volkswagen have an active interest and participation in rotary engine programmes, through their respective interests in Citroen and NSU.

Financial and motor industry experts believe that eventually the European motor industry will be reduced to fewer than five major companies — certainly few experts expect there to be more than three firms manufacturing cars in quantity by the end of the century.

In Britain the most remarkable success story of the 1960s was that of the Ford Motor Company. When they introduced the 105E Anglia in 1959 they moved straight from their image as builders of archaic hangovers from the 1930s into the 1960s. The Anglia was followed by the Classic, which was not as successful, then the Cortina, Corsair, the small Escort to replace the Anglia, and the sporty Capri. None of their cars were technically advanced, apart from having strong, high revving engines and robust gearboxes, but their clever styling and sporting potential were strong sales points; Ford captured nearly 30 per cent of the British market.

The British Leyland Motor Corporation which had committed itself to a policy of advanced engineering with the Mini, 1100, 1800, Maxi and 2200 suddenly revised their programme and introduced a thoroughly conventional car, the Marina, which went from the drawing board to production in little more than 18 months instead of the usual three to five years. This car featured the torsion bar front suspension from the Morris Minor, which in effect it replaced, together with a rigid rear axle on semi elliptic leaf springs. Engines used were the long lived 1275 cc 'A' and 1798 cc 'B' series units, which dated back to the first Morris Minor of 1948. Concocted to meet a market need, this car was clothed in an attractive looking body and was intended to compete with the successful Ford Cortina and Hillman Avenger models which were dominating sales to fleet and hire car operators. In this it enjoyed some success yet made no great impression on the overall market despite reaching a production level of 4,000 cars a week, which gave it 8 per cent of the British market. It did not fare well in export markets because it offered few if any advantages over home produced vehicles.

Apart from British Leyland's front wheel drive cars, the British industry relied almost entirely on conventional vehicles for the mass-produced market. However, as always specialist makers of sports and quality cars upheld British prestige. In 1961 Jaguar Cars announced their E-Type, a logical successor to the XK120 of 1948; this sensational car with a monocoque chassis based on the D-type sports/racing car was powered by the ubiquitous XK twin-overhead camshaft six cylinder engine which gave it 150 mph capability. Its superb looks complemented the performance and handling, and Jaguar had great difficulty in coping with demand.

The first E-type used the 3·8 litre

Opposite, top: **the four wheel-drive Jensen FF which was in production from 1966 until 1971. The Lotus Elan (*centre*) and the Mercedes 280SL (*left*). The pretty, but unsuccessful, the 2600 Sprint coupé Alfa Romeo (*top*), and the BMW 2800 CS coupé (*above*).**

engine, which was succeeded by the 4·2 litre in 1964, while in 1971 the long awaited V12 engined version appeared. In the early 1960s Jaguar had built an experimental mid-engined sports/racing car powered by a twin overhead camshaft V12 engine giving over 500 bhp, but this car was abandoned when the company decided not to re-enter racing. However, the idea of a V12 engine was not discarded and in 1971 a single overhead camshaft per bank versions was announced. This 5·3 litre engine gave 272 bhp and complied with all the American pollution regulations — otherwise it would be capable of producing at least 350 bhp. The Series 3 E-type has a longer wheelbase and the V12 gives it a top speed of over 140 mph.

The Jaguar XJ6 announced in 1969 was a five-seater saloon using the XK six-cylinder engine and was adjudged by experts to be outstanding in its class; like all of Sir William Lyon's Jaguars, it coupled refinement with surprisingly low catalogued

prices — qualities which assured a steady demand even during periods when the rest of the motor industry suffered the efforts of recession. It was followed in 1972 by the XJ12, the XJ6 body shell with the V12 engine filling the engine compartment — a certain recipe for success. It was the only four-door V12 engined car to be built in quantity for decades.

Rolls-Royce continued to make superb cars despite the setback in 1971 when the aero engine side of the business was forced into liquidation. Demand for the Rolls-Royce Silver Shadow, especially from the Americans, continued unabated and the factory was unable to keep pace with the demand, despite the high prices of all its models, especially the coach-built Corniche version which costs nearly £13,000.

There was still advanced engineering to be seen and bought, for Jensen developed and produced the FF, which at the time was the only road-going car, as distinct from a vehicle with cross-country capability, to use four-wheel drive. This was the Ferguson system, which was also used on experimental vehicles supplied to police forces, but in the FF it was coupled with the Dunlop Maxaret anti-lock braking system.

The ingenious Range Rover was the most successful compromise yet achieved in a car between off-road

capability and highway cruising qualities — its 3½ litre V8 engine drove through all four wheels to give excellent cross-country performance, while it had a smooth road top speed of 100 mph, with a standard of comfort far removed from that of Rover's utilitarian Land Rover. The same V8 engine was used in the Rover 3500, which in most other respects derived from the 2000; this model had been regarded as something of a *tour de force* when it was announced in 1964, for it featured an unusual front suspension, de Dion rear axle, and a single overhead camshaft bowl-in-piston engine.

Colin Chapman's Lotus company became outstanding among the smaller specialist manufacturers during the 1960s, especially when the Elan superseded the Elite. The Elan was a small sports car in its dimensions and in the manner in which it could be driven, yet in smoothness of ride it was far removed from the 'traditional' British sports car (typified through the decade by the evergreen Morgans, and by the stark Lotus Seven, for which demand obstinately continued after the factory had announced its demise). The rear-engined Lotus Europa appeared in 1967, and was transformed into a car to satisfy enthusiasts in 1971 when its original Renault engine was replaced with Lotus' race-proved twin-ohc 1·6 litre unit.

On the Continent, Citroen continued to lead the world in suspension design when their ID/DS of the 1950s were joined by the award winning GS and SM in 1970. The GS is a small car featuring the famous Citroen self-levelling hydro-pneumatic suspension and powered by a 1 litre engine which drives the front wheels. The SM is a large four-seater sports saloon powered by a Maserati designed and built V6 engine which again drives the front wheels. Suspension is similar to that of the DS and GS series. In a country which taxes cars over 2·8 litres very heavily the 2·6 litre SM is very popular because it is France's only remaining prestige car.

In Germany the hold Mercedes had retained on the high priced saloon car market was weakened in the late 1960s by BMW, a company which had been on the verge of bankruptcy at the turn of the decade. Then they had been building expensive motorcycles, the Isetta bubble car and the small 700 saloon, but a brand new saloon, the 1500, which

Above: the Javelin rescued American Motors from financial trouble and this later AMX model made a successful sortie into the TransAm saloon car racing series. *Opposite:* Jaguar revealed their very sophisticated XJ12 saloon in 1972. Its 5 litre engine powers the car smoothly to a top speed of 140 mph.

was rapidly followed by the 1600, 1800 and 2000 soon became popular in Germany and when big six-cylinder 2500, 2800 and 3 litre models were added to the range, BMW became a forceful rival to Mercedes.

In America the increasing support that the Japanese cars were receiving could hardly be ignored by the home industry, which found that many buyers were not using small foreign cars as second cars but as their first and only vehicle.

In an attempt to combat this trend, American manufacturers again turned to the compact car. Ford were first in this field with the Maverick which was not really very compact, but they followed it up with the Pinto, a smaller car powered by a 2-litre overhead camshaft engine (many of the mechanical components of the Pinto

were made in Ford's British and German plants, and the engine is used in Ford European models).

Chevrolet then produced the Vega, another 2 litre car, while American Motors quickly developed the Gremlin, which resembled a very much shortened version of their AMX sports coupé. These conventional front-engined, rear-drive cars made little immediate impact on the sales of imported cars, partly because they are larger than the small Japanese and German cars which formed bulk of imports. With current USA safety legislation demanding a burden of heavy crash resistant features, the small car may in any case be doomed on the American market.

Past experience suggests that the trends in America will eventually percolate through to Europe, for the old

adage that 'when America sneezes England catches a cold' has been remarkably accurate on many occasions. Out of town speed limits of 70 mph were imposed in England in 1968, France and Belgium followed suit in imposing main road speed limits, Germany has partially imposed speed limits and only Italy of the major motor manufacturing countries in Europe has no speed limits out of towns, although with the high price of petrol in that country few drivers are encouraged to drive fast! Pollution and safety legislation is being imposed throughout Europe.

The short term future looks bleak for motor manufacturers and motorists, but worse problems have been overcome in the past. The best builders will survive to build fine cars for enthusiasts to drive.

HIGH PERFORMANCE AND REFINEMENT

The majority of motorists drive ordinary mass-produced cars, identical with hundreds of thousands of others, but there is a desire in most people to drive an individual and distinctive car. Whether it is the Walter Mitty in us or simply the desire to appear better than one's neighbour is a question that could only be answered by a psychologist, but there are many thousands of drivers who just want to be different. Those motorists who are not sufficiently affluent to buy an expensive car often modify their more humble machine by fitting special wheels, tuning the engine for better performance, painting it an unusual colour or merely by painting a stripe down the middle. The art of customising, as it is known in America, is spreading rapidly but it is not fully satisfying for the car underneath is still a relatively inexpensive mass-produced machine. Many people attempt a kind of reverse snobbery, such as building a cheap beach buggy or paying thousands of pounds to modify a Mini in every conceivable way, but the only way to express true wealth and discernment is to buy an expensive car.

Between the two world wars the rich had an almost unlimited choice of refined conveyances, for the majority of luxury cars were built as chassis only, complete with running gear. The buyer purchased his Rolls-Royce, Hispano-Suiza, Bentley or Isotta-Fraschini chassis then sent it to his favourite coachbuilder for the body to be fitted. Many of the bodies were standard designs but special coachwork could be built at extra cost.

After the Second World War rapid development of the unit construction car, in which the body and chassis were stamped out of steel panels and welded together, almost put an end to the coachbuilding trade, and firms such as James Young, Vanden Plas, Tickford, Thrupp and Maberley, Mulliner, Park Ward in England, Brewster in America and many of the French and Italian coachbuilders were forced to close or turn to other work. In England, only H. J. Mulliner continues to build special bodies on Rolls-Royces, now as a subsidiary of Rolls-Royce. Vanden Plas was taken over by BMC, and used as a 'badge-engineering' make name, and James Young is a Fiat agency in Bromley, although they do still undertake some coachwork repairs. Harold Radford, the former Bentley and Rolls-Royce coachbuilder gained new fame by building very expensive Minis for pop stars.

The place of the traditional coachbuilders who usually built large bodies on expensive chassis was gradually taken over by small specialists who generally concentrated on bodies for sports and grand touring cars. This trade flourished most prominently in Italy, where large numbers of *carozzeria* sprang up after the Second World War, and many developed into full-scale manufacturers. The best known are Bertone and Pininfarina, but numerous others like Vignale, Touring, Michelotti, Frua, Osi, Scagliatti, Fissore, Zagato, Ghia, Italdesign, Moretti, Coggiola and Coriasco appeared; many of them equally quickly faded away again, mainly because of the expense of building special bodies on cars which were of unit construction. However, several of them still exist today, relying for much of their business on commissioned styling exercises for the large manufacturers. Bertone and Pininfarina design bodies for Fiat, Ferrari, Lancia and Peugeot; Pininfarina were responsible for the 'Farina-line' Austin A40, A60 and Morris Oxford of the late 1950s, and Michelotti designed numerous bodies for Triumph, including the TR4, Herald and Vitesse models. Many Japanese and American firms retained Italian stylists to work for them and the great improvement in American car styling dates from the time that Italian body-builders were engaged. Strangely, one of the most stylish American makes, Studebaker, with their handsome Hawk and later sporting Avanti, suffered badly from poor sales and eventually went into liquidation.

Many of the pre-war marques which provided luxury motoring for the rich and famous failed to survive the austerity conditions of the late 1940s — names such as Bugatti, Hispano-Suiza Delahaye, Delage, Hotchkiss, Invicta, Railton either failed to return after the war or lingered for only a few years. In America, the classic marques like Stutz, Pierce-Arrow, Duesenberg, Cord, Auburn and Marmon were long since gone.

Fortunately, when the privations of post-war Europe were overcome, new marques began to appear. Many of them, like France's Facel Vega and Spain's Pegaso, were doomed to eventual failure, but they brightened an otherwise gloomy period.

Perhaps the most glamorous marque to rise after the war was Ferrari. The name of Scuderia Ferrari was already well known before the war, when Enzo Ferrari had run the official Alfa Romeo racing team, but after the war he commenced building his own cars, from the first using a V12 engine. The V12 soon became a

The Ford Mustang revolutionised American motoring in 1964, for it was the first sporty 'pony car' to catch on. This is a 1973 model.

Ferrari trade mark and for many years, until the V6 Dino engine was announced, the factory built nothing but V12s.

The first 'street' Ferraris were light, stark two-seater sports cars, but the first to become really familiar was the 250GT series, soon sought after by wealthy connoisseurs. For many years the 250GT remained a relatively conventional design, the V12 engine being front mounted, driving through a five-speed gearbox to a rigid rear axle, but later models incorporated independent rear suspension, disc brakes, even air conditioning and other apurtenances of gracious living. Among related V12 models was the 410 super, the 275GTB and GTS, the 330GT and the 365 — the 365GTB4 Daytona model is one of the world's fastest Grand Touring cars, easily topping 170 mph. For this sort of performance you will have to lay down nearly £10,000, but half of this will buy the little V6 mid-engined Dino Ferrari, which is capable of around 140 mph.

After the war the Maserati brothers sold their firm to Count Orsi, under whom Maserati turned from a manufacturer of pure racing machines to build a fascinating range of racing and touring cars. The 3500GT was the first real road car to make an impression, the straight six twin overhead camshaft engine giving the car a top speed of over 130 mph. Speed gradually increased, while the factory supplemented the straight six with a brand new V8 developed from

a racing engine. The range was expanded to include models like the Sebring, Mistral and Quattroporte — their first four-door four-seater — and the Ghibli, which has a claim to be the most beautiful front-engined car ever built. The body was designed by Giorgetto Giugiaro, who has subsequently built many exciting cars and has formed his own design company called Italdesign. Maserati's latest offering is the Bora, a mid-engined two-seater very similar to Ferrari's Berlinetta Boxer (the Bora uses the well-known V8 engine whereas the Ferrari uses a 4·5 litre flat 12 engine developed from their flat 12 racing engine).

A post-war phenomenon in Italy was Lamborghini. Ferruccio Lamborghini followed the traditional rags to riches trail, building up a tractor empire from nothing after the war. The story goes that he was once kept waiting by Enzo Ferrari when he went to buy a Ferrari, so he returned to Bologna in a rage and decided to make his own car. His first car, designed by a young man called Gian Paulo Dallara, was a sensation because it featured a brand new V12 engine designed by Bizzarini, the equal of anything that Ferrari had made, and its tough chassis had full independent suspension at a time when Ferrari was still using a rigid rear axle. The Lamborghini 350GT, as the first car was called, was followed by the 400GT. Then Lamborghini astonished the motoring world by announcing the Miura, a low slung two-seater with a 4 litre V12 engine installed sideways behind the cockpit. In conception this sleek machine was very reminiscent of contemporary racing machinery yet it was

a tractable car which could be driven on the road and is still one of the fastest road cars in the world — if not the fastest. The Miura was followed by the Islero, a front-engined four-seater, then the Espada, another front-engined four-seater, with sensational styling. The Jarama replaced the Islero in 1971 and a brand new 2½ litre four-seater coupé, the Urraco, was added to the range. The Urraco's engine was also set across the car at the rear like the Miura and this small car was designed to compete with Porsche, selling for around £5,000.

However, the Italian specialists faced considerable problems as the cost of manufacture steadily increased and orders for cars declined during periods of financial depression. Ferrari rebuffed an offer from Ford of America, then sold out to Fiat; Maserati was bought by Citroen and Lamborghini sold a 51 per cent interest to a Swiss watchmaking tycoon, not because his car factory was in trouble, but because his tractor business was as a result of a world wide slump in sales (he was forced to sell his tractor factory to Fiat). Several small Italian companies barely managed to maintain production, and some of them ceased business. Bizzarini built a number of coupés powered by American Chevrolet V8s, Iso still build the Grifo and Rivolta models powered by Chrysler V8s, Abarth built a number of small high-powered coupés, but were eventually taken over by Fiat.

One man who eventually succeeded was the mercurial Argentinian Alessandro de Tomaso. He designed a number of interesting machines which never got into production because he lost interest in them. But

Top: the 911 Porsche has gained many racing and rallying successes, giving Sobieslaw Zasada the European rally championship. The ultimate version of the 911 is the 2·7 litre Carrera (*above*). The Lamborghini Urraco (*below*) was intended as a rival to Porsche.

with the Mangusta, using a rear-mounted American Ford V8 engine, he found a formula for success, although the Mangusta had many problems connected with its road-holding. It was superseded by the Pantera (Panther), and with the problems cured this sold well, especially in America. De Tomaso and his associated body building company of Ghia was taken over in 1970 by Ford, who undertook marketing in the USA (Ford had previously marketed the British built Ford GT40 but this was virtually a racing car and had a very limited market).

Another American firm to turn to Italy for a mid-engined GT car was American Motors, who commissioned a GT car from Giotto Bizzarini, who had earlier designed the Lamborghini engine. The car used American Motors suspension and mechanical parts where possible, including the 6·3 litre V8 engine mated to a ZF gearbox, but after two or three prototypes had been built American Motors lost interest.

Elsewhere in Europe, the spirit of adventure flourished only occasionally, most manufacturers preferring to build solid, dependable and profitable machines. In Germany only Mercedes indulged in the occasional extravagance; their 300SL ranks as an all time classic because it bore so many resemblances to the racing Mercedes coupés. With a straight six 240 bhp fuel injected 3 litre engine mounted in a tubular steel chassis it was one of the fastest production sports cars of the 1950s and its gull-wing doors were a novel and very attractive feature. However, high production costs limited its life and thereafter Mercedes concentrated on less exotic machinery until in 1970 they announced the C111, a futuristic coupé powered by a triple rotor Wankel engine and capable of over 140 mph. It never went into production and is regarded as a mobile test bed for future rotary engines designed to go into production saloon.

Porsche of Stuttgart have built nothing but sports cars, their beautifully constructed flat-four and flat-six engines giving the cars remarkable performance from small engine capacities. The largest production Porsche engine is the 2·4 litre unit of the 911 (although a flat-12 5 litre engine was used to power the 917 Prototype racing car).

In France the tax system legislates against large engines and the interesting cars built by the coach-

Volkswagen-based beach buggies
and sports coupés gained a brief
vogue during the late '60s, but
increasingly stringent legislation
tends to force them off the roads.
In this group are a Silhouette, a
Centron and a Siva, all of which
used VW chassis.

building firm of Facel Vega lasted only a few years before they were forced to close down. These big cars, powered by American Chrysler V8s have since become collectors' items. Facel Vega also built a small car powered by their own engine but this proved very unreliable and was replaced by a Volvo unit.

Switzerland has fathered few car manufacturers, but in the last few years a Basle BMW dealer, Peter Monteverdi, has constructed a series of high performance saloons and GT cars. The Monteverdi uses Chrysler engines and transmissions in a chassis of Swiss design which uses mainly English suspension and brake parts. The bodies are designed and built in Italy and the models available include two- and four-door front-engined cars

and the Hai (shark), a mid-engined coupé – the bellow of a Chrysler Hemi positioned just behind the driver is quite frightening!

In Britain the high performance GT car has continued to flourish despite the sort of Government legislation which would have deterred constructors who were not determined men. Aston Martin has survived numerous financial crises and is still in production; after the war David Brown, later Sir David, bought up the ailing company and started production with the DB1 and followed up quickly with the DB2/4, DB3 and the DB4, 5 and 6 before supplementing the 6 with the DBS, which became available with a 5 litre V8 engine in 1970. This 160 mph car proved popular with a small discerning band

Aston Martin gained many racing successes but their DB4GT and 212 prototype could seldom match contemporary Ferraris.

of supporters but the company lost money on each car and in 1972 the David Brown group sold the company to a financial group who continued to build the DBS. Aston Martin had been staunch motor racing competitors for many years and in 1959 they won the World Sports Car Championship with the DBR/1, which had a straight six twin-overhead camshaft engine very similar to that used in the production

The AC 428 was developed directly from the 7 litre AC Cobra, the body being made by Vignale in Italy.

The Chevrolet Corvette Sting Ray is an American sports car, but its existence in this form has been threatened by safety legislation.

cars. The group also made Lagonda cars for a time but these were unprofitable and soon dropped (a racing Lagonda V12 was built in 1954 but this 300 bhp, 4·4 litre engine was never successful in competition).

AC, the small Thames-side car builders, carried on with an interesting range of sports and GT cars after the war, eventually turning to the 2 litre Bristol engine in the 1950s. The AC Ace and Aceca are now

Built primarily for racing, the Dodge Charger Daytona is an eye-catching road car by any standards.

popular classics and fetch high prices when they come on the market, but the name of AC really became noticed world wide when American driver Carroll Shelby selected the AC chassis for use as the basis of a sports car which he developed in conjunction with Ford of America. Initially a 4·7 litre Ford V8 engine was mounted in a slightly modified Ace chassis, but later on a new chassis with coil springs in place of transverse leaf springs was specified and a 7 litre V8 engine was fitted. This thundering monster, the Cobra, was greatly prized among enthusiasts and over 2000 were built before production ceased in 1968, when American safety laws made it impossible to import the car into the USA. Highly tuned versions were used in racing

and the works team of Cobras won the World GT Championship in 1965. In England a Cobra hit the newspaper headlines when the factory tested a racing model on the M1 Motorway soon after dawn one summer morning. It was timed at 190 mph and the police were not amused, even though at that time there were no speed limits in England.

When their contract to build Cobras finished AC took the chassis used on the 7 litre, extended the wheelbase slightly and fitted it with a steel body built by Frua of Italy, in place of the light alloy sports body of the Cobra. The 428, as the new model was called, appeared in both convertible and coupé forms and will top 140 mph on the road.

Many British small series manu-

Left, top to bottom: the Jaguar V12 E type, the de Tomaso Pantera, the Pontiac Firebird and the Alfa Romeo Montreal. *Above:* Pontiac Firebird.

facturers turned to American V8s as a quick means to economical power, a trend which started in the 1930s. Among these were Allard, Bristol, Jensen, AC, TVR, Ginetta, and Trident while Rover and Morgan used the Rover built version of the Buick 3·5 litre V8, and Rolls-Royce and Daimler went over to V8 engines which were inspired by American practice. Allard achieved a brief vogue in the States, especially with their hairy J2X model which was powered by a Mercury 'flathead' but the company was forced out of production by more sophisticated competitive models and sheer economics. The Bristol, built by the Bristol Aeroplane Company, was originally powered by their own 2 litre engine but this was later replaced by a Chrysler V8 when more power was needed. The latest 411 model is a 130 mph machine and although it is no longer built by Bristol, the quality remains.

Jensen was originally a coachbuilding firm but the Jensen brothers turned to building complete cars with a degree of success. The company survived various financial problems, gaining some stability through contracts to build Austin-Healey and Sunbeam Tiger bodies. However, the Jensen Interceptor 2+2 model announced in 1967 was the real turning point, for the Chrysler V8 engined

car was immediately successful. The more expensive FF with four-wheel drive and Dunlop Maxaret anti-locking brakes also sold to a discerning few. An American, Carl Duerr, put the company on its feet financially, then in 1971 the Norwegian born, American domiciled, Kjell Qvale bought a controlling interest. Under his guidance, Jensen undertook production of the Jensen-Healey, a small sports car powered by the Lotus 2 litre engine. This marked the return of Donald Healey to car building, and with his son he was responsible for the initial design of the car. A 'traditional' front-engined sports car, it is aimed above all at the American market, the majority being sold through Qvale's American company, British Motor Distributors, which handles a large proportion of the British sports cars sold in America.

Although Jaguars are competitively priced they still fit into the luxury category for the V12 engine of the latest E-type enables it to top 140 mph with ease and accelerate to 100 mph as fast as most of the specialist cars built by Ferrari or Aston Martin. The Jaguar is frowned on by some buyers of fast cars purely because it is seen in large numbers and they feel there is not so much prestige to be gained in driving a car which is seen so often on the road that it rarely rates a second glance.

Small manufacturers: Sydney Allard built exciting sports cars around American engines; this one (*above*) is competing in an Alpine Rally. The Gilbern Invader (*opposite top*) is the only car made in Wales. The Clan Crusader (*right*) uses Hillman Imp parts.

Outside of England and Italy there are few really expensive luxury cars in production. In America, where demand is highest, labour charges are so high that it is relatively uneconomic to build specialised cars. The few cars available are either replicas of pre-war classics like the Excalibur, which is a copy of the Mercedes SSK, the Cord 812, Duesenberg SJ or special bodies on standard chassis like the 'Stutz Black Hawk', which utilises a Cadillac chassis.

For anyone who wants a true dream car that nobody else in the world possess, the only solution is to go to Italy. Here the art of special one-off coachbuilding still flourishes, but even in Italy where labour is relatively cheap, the cost of having a special car built is astronomical. However, the annual Turin show, held every November, still turns up the glamorous confections which bodybuilders often build in the hope that a manufacturer will buy the design. And even if they do not sell, it is pleasant to dream about that dream car.

Right: the only Swiss car manufacturer is Monteverdi, who builds big GT cars such as this 375L powered by Chrysler engines.
Below: the Aston Martin DBS V8 was intended to be Britain's 160 mph answer to the Ferrari.
Opposite, top: the gull wing Mercedes Benz 300SL of the mid-1950s is one of the all time great cars.
Opposite, bottom: the Ferrari Lusso, a characteristically purposeful car built by this most famous of Italian manufacturers.

THE TOUGHEST PROVING GROUND

After the Second World War the popularity of motor sport increased dramatically. One reason was perhaps that a flood of reasonably affluent young men who had acquired a taste for danger and adventure were released into civilian life. The natural outlet for many of them was to drive racing cars.

During the 1930s racing was largely an amateur sport, only the wealthy being able to afford the necessary machinery to win races. Prize money was low and only in Germany and Italy were racing teams run on a professional footing, largely because Hitler and Mussolini saw them as means to bolster national pride. In America road racing was virtually unknown between the wars, although board track, midget and Indianapolis racing was very popular.

By the early 1950s motor sport was in a period of unprecedented boom. Manufacturers were beginning to realise the vast publicity benefits accruing from success in competition, as well as the excellent development ground it provided for their cars. Italy dominated early postwar motor racing with Alfa Romeo, Maserati and Ferrari, but many British firms joined in and soon began to win, at first mainly in sports car events. Jaguar started to race with their C-type, which was followed by the D-type and the company notched up five prestigious victories at Le Mans. Aston Martin, too, entered sports car racing and although less successful than Jaguar they won the 1959 World Sports Car Championship and developed their six-cylinder, twin-overhead camshaft engine, which powered all road-going Aston Martins until it was superseded by the V8 in 1971.

The Mercedes W196 of 1954–5 swept the board in Grand Prix racing (Juan Manuel Fangio and Stirling Moss in the 1955 Dutch GP at Zandvoort).

In 1954 Mercedes-Benz, who had already built a successful sports racing car, announced their return to Formula 1 racing, with Juan Manuel Fangio as their leading driver in 1954, backed up by Stirling Moss in 1955. The German cars dominated racing for these two seasons before Mercedes retired from competition. Many of the lessons the company learned in racing were incorporated in the saloon and sporting cars which they produced in the subsequent two decades and, of course, the prestige of success lingered.

With the retirement of Mercedes, Ferrari and Maserati resumed their winning ways for a year or two, but British Racing Green was looming large in the shape of BRM, Connaught, Vanwall, Cooper and Lotus. Soon the world's premier single seater races were being won by British cars driven by British drivers like Stirling Moss and Tony Brooks and later on by Graham Hill, Jim Clark and Jackie Stewart. These victories enhanced the prestige of British motor engineering abroad and aided the development of brakes, clutches, fuel injection, tyres and electrical equipment.

When the large manufacturers began to discover that the costs of participation had started to outweigh the benefits many of them withdrew, leaving the field to small, specialist constructors who relied on sponsorship from fuel and tyre companies, cigarette and cosmetic manufacturers. Names like Brabham, March, Tyrrell, McLaren and Lola began to appear in entry lists, firms whose only product was racing cars. These teams are in competition with only slightly less specialised companies like Lotus, Ferrari, Matra and

Jack Brabham in his Brabham-Repco leading Jim Clark's Lotus-Climax in 1966. Jack Brabham won the World Championship in 1966, the first man to win with a car of his own make.

Alfa Romeo, who also produce road cars.

Generally, the larger European manufacturers turned to production car racing and rallying in the 1950s and 1960s because the public could more easily identify themselves with the cars which looked outwardly like the ones the man in the street could buy, although underneath, their tuned engines, strengthened chassis, stiffened suspensions and so on were very different and could be very expensive.

The 1950s was the great era of the classic long distance road rallies like the Monte Carlo, Liège—Rome—Liège, Coupe des Alpes and the Acropolis, where sheer speed and endurance determined the winner. These rallies were fought out between the major manufacturers, each one advertising his victories to the full in newspapers. The British Motor Corporation was a staunch supporter of rallies, their Austin-Healey 3000 being a popular car for the long distance events, although in the 1960s

the Mini Cooper was for several years a popular rally weapon. Mercedes, Porsche, Lancia, Saab and Ford contested the big rallies with honours swaying fairly evenly. The tough Swedish Saab was designed for the rough roads of Scandinavia and the burly Erik Carlsson was often to be seen winning the big rallies of the late 1950s and early 1960s.

But increasing traffic in Europe led to difficulties over the use of roads — even some of the formerly little used roads in Yugoslavia and the Italian Alps became busy in the summer and the police began to restrict rallies, to the extent that many of them disappeared from the calendar. The Liège—Rome—Liège was turned into a motor race at the Nürburgring, the Coupe des Alpes was abandoned and the Monte-Carlo rally is a shadow of its former self. The emphasis turned to off-road rallying, with the really fast and competitive motoring taking place on private roads or in forests. Britain's popular RAC rally, held every November, set the pattern in this, as the tests of speed take place mainly on Forestry Commission land, and thus cause no inconvenience to the public.

Nevertheless, the increasing cost of taking part in rallies reduced fac-

tory participation tremendously. After the British Leyland Motor Corporation was formed, companies within that colossus withdrew from rallying, and from racing, leaving Ford as the sole major British competitor. Even Ford began to ration their appearances, only taking part in events where they were likely to do well or those which received a great deal of publicity.

The really long distance events like the London to Sydney Marathon and the World Cup Rally boosted rallying for a short spell, and did a good deal to boost the reputations of Hillman and Ford respectively, as

The Austin-Healey 3000 made a fine name for itself in International rallying during the 1960s.

Top: Jackie Stewart won the 1971 World Championship in his Tyrrell-Ford; in 1972 when he was troubled by illness and by unreliability in a new Tyrrell was runner-up to Brazilian Emerson Fittipaldi.

Left: the World Championship in 1972 went to a relative newcomer, Emerson Fittipaldi, who drove the John Player Special Lotus to victory in five Grands Prix.

Right: the Porsche 917 won the Sports car Championship in 1970 and 1971. In 1971 the British John Wyer team, sponsored by the Gulf fuel company, won the championship with these classic sports-racing cars.

they won the events, but the expense and numerous difficulties of running these marathons has virtually finished them. Ford capitalised on their World Cup victory with the Mexico high performance version of the Escort, which is loosely based on the winning car, and put into small scale production at Ford's Advanced Vehicle Operation.

One rally to which great kudos is attached is the East African Safari. The majority of the roads in Kenya, Uganda and Tanzania where the rally is held are loose dirt, often feet deep in water, and any car which even reaches the finish is very tough indeed. Traditionally the event has been won by Peugeot or Volvo, and usually by a local driver, but in 1972 Ford won the rally with an RS1600 Escort driven by Hannu Mikola and Gunnar Palm. The victory undoubtedly enhanced Ford's reputation in Africa, where sales are based very much on victories in events like the Safari.

Saloon car racing in Europe developed after the war when near-standard machines would lurch around circuits at modest speeds. Spectators enjoyed the spectacle and soon all sorts of classes were devised ranging from those for near-standard saloons which had been produced at the rate of at least 5,000 a year to near-racing cars where practically everything could be changed to obtain more performance. Jaguar dominated most of these races until one or two drivers introduced cars like Ford Galaxies and Chevrolets to England; these 7 litre machines soon disposed of the 3·8 litre Jaguars. There was much interest in class battles and there was great rivalry between Minis, Imps and Anglias in the 1000 cc class. As the racing became more professional and more expensive some makes dropped out until only Ford, BMW, Alfa Romeo and Porsche participated regularly, but in the early 1970s Porsche retired, leaving Alfa Romeo, Ford and BMW as the only real protagonists. The Ford Escort with the four valve per cylinder Cosworth designed engine became very difficult to beat, save on the fastest circuits — even Chevrolet Camaro and Ford Mustang

Top: **Briggs Cunningham was one of the few Americans to build sports cars for racing. This is the C2R. A. J. Foyt in the last front-engined car to win at Indianapolis (***centre***) which contrasts with the 1971 Indianapolis McLaren.**

drivers found difficulty in holding the Escorts on the slower tracks. Many motorists feel that the highly tuned saloons have little in common with the cars they drive on the road and the result was a move towards Group 1 racing, in which near standard cars can show their paces.

In America road racing began to gain a hold when the sports car craze arrived in 1947. Soon sports car races were being held all over the USA and this in turn led to American drivers making international names for themselves. Phil Hill joined Ferrari and became World Champion in 1961, Richie Ginther drove for several teams, including Ferrari, BRM and Honda, Dan Gurney drove for Ferrari, Porsche and Brabham then built his own Formula 1 car, called the Eagle after the American national emblem. Other American constructors had earlier built cars to race in Europe, the most notable being Briggs Cunningham and Lance Reventlow. Cunningham wanted to win the Le Mans 24-hour Race for America; he spent a lot of money trying to, but he never quite made it, third place being the best he could manage. Reventlow, heir to the Woolworth fortune, first of all built a very successful sports racing car then the Scarab Formula 1 single seater which he brought to Europe. Unfortunately his car used a front mounted engine at a time when the faster cars were using rear engines and the Scarab was not competitive.

Despite the upsurge in road racing interest, the most popular forms of racing in America were for the Indianapolis style single seaters, which raced almost exclusively on banked oval tracks. The cars were very specialised, and few Europeans even knew what type of cars raced at Indianapolis until John Cooper took a Formula 1 Cooper to the track for Jack Brabham to drive. Brabham found that the mid-engined Cooper went round corners much faster than the lumbering front engined 'roadsters' and although he had only a 2·7 litre Coventry-Climax engine compared with the 4·2 litre engines of the American cars he finished a comfortable ninth overall in the 1961 race. This set Dan Gurney and Colin Chapman of Lotus thinking and they approached Ford with the proposition that the American company back an attack on the '500' with cars initially using ordinary production 4·2 litre Ford V8 engines. Eventually they

agreed and Chapman produced a mid-engined car for the 1963 race. Driven by Jim Clark the Lotus almost won, but misunderstood regulations meant that he eventually finished second. The engine was only giving about 350 bhp, at a time when the Offenhauser engines were giving over 400 bhp, but the Lotus used less fuel and was able to make fewer pit stops during the 500-mile race.

Ford really became interested in winning at Indianapolis and for 1964 a new twin overhead camshaft engine was produced. Again Clark failed to win, this time because of tyre trouble. Finally, Clark won the

1965 race for Lotus and Ford. By that time most cars were rear engined and using Ford engines, which for a while put the venerable Offenhauser out of contention. Soon, American constructors and drivers got the hang of rear-engined cars and although Graham Hill won the 1966 race in a Lola, American drivers scooped the big prizes from then on, with A. J. Foyt, the Unser brothers and the Italian born Mario Andretti winning. The technical aspect of Indianapolis had stagnated for years, but suddenly no innovation was too ingenious for the Speedway. Four-wheel drive was used as a matter of course and in

1967 the gas turbine engine came to Indianapolis. Using a turbine powered car Parnelli Jones almost won and soon several other turbine cars were running in 'Indy style' races. They would have eventually swamped the piston engined cars, but the rules were changed to limit their power output and these changes effectively ruled the turbine out of contention.

There had been an agreement between the three major American manufacturers not to take part in motor racing but when Ford realised the great benefits to be obtained from motor sport they opted out of the agreement and began sponsoring

cars for all types of racing and rallying. They built engines for Indianapolis cars, they used Ford Falcons in European rallies, they sponsored the Cobra, they built the GT40 and Mk 2 and Mk 4 GT coupés, they supported drag racing and supplied cars for stock car racing in America. Not only that but their European subsidiaries were encouraged to support racing and rallying. Perhaps the best investment of all was the £100,000 which Ford of Britain made in Cosworth Engineering, to design and build a 3 litre engine for the new Formula 1 which started in 1966. Without this engine many British teams would have been virtually forced to withdraw from racing as no other suitable engine was available, and moreover the Ford Cosworth DFV dominated Grand Prix racing for five years. Ford

or Ford-based engines have been used in almost all the successful single seaters in Europe, certainly in the international Formulae 1, 2 and 3.

The effect of Ford's success was not lost on General Motors, and although they officially deny any connection with racing it is generally believed that they gave much support to the very successful Chaparral cars which won many sports car races using Chevrolet engines and automatic transmissions. The successes of Chevrolet in stock car and drag racing events was further evidence of GM's interest.

Another form of racing came about soon after the medium sized American 'pony cars' were introduced. The Sports Car Club of America announced the Trans-Am series for saloon cars with engines of 5-litres.

Above: after many years of trying a European team finally won the East African Safari in 1972. The winning Ford Escort BDA was driven by Hannu Mikkola and Gunnar Palm. The Ford GT40 (*above, right*) was one of the most successful GT cars of all time. Here the winning car in the Le Mans 24-hour race of 1968 makes a routine pit stop. Stock car racing is one of the most popular sports in America. *Right:* the field in the Daytona 500 gets under way.

This became an immediate success, for the public flocked to see road races starring the pony cars. The battle between the Chevrolet Camaros, Ford Mustangs, Plymouth Barracudas and American Motors Javelins see-sawed over the seasons, first one than the other getting the upper hand. The factories seldom entered their own teams but usually paid other specialised racing car teams to run cars for them. The best team usually won races whichever cars they were running, and the Parnelli Jones and Roger Penske teams proved to be most successful, Jones running Fords and Penske first Camaros then Javelins. The manufacturers realised the importance of these races and for a few seasons spent a great deal of money sponsoring teams.

Ford of America finally decided to reduce their direct involvement in motor racing and gradually pulled out of various forms of racing, but not before they had shown just what a large manufacturer can do if a great deal of money is available. Several Indianapolis victories came their way as well as a number of stock car wins, a pair of Le Mans successes with their Mk. 2 and Mk. 4 sports racing cars (and two more gained by the Gulf-backed John Wyer team of GT40s).

Meanwhile, racing engines sponsored by Ford of Britain, or based on their production units had powered the cars that gained scores of victories in Formula 1 and 2 racing, and hundreds in Formula 3 and other single-seater classes; their outwardly standard saloons had scored innumerable rally and race victories, at every level from prestigious international events to minor club competitions.

Rallying has never been popular in the USA because of restricted driving conditions and low speed limits so many drivers who are not rich enough to go racing have turned to drag racing; many take their cars along to local drag strips to see how fast they can go. Literally thousands of these drag strips exist and most nights any driver can drive his road car along the timed quarter-mile strip to see if his car is quicker than the next man's.

Another form of racing which has become popular is off-road racing which takes place in the deserts of California and other West coast states. It all started with the Volkswagen based Beach Buggies which were quickly developed to be very rapid cross-country vehicles. Drivers soon began to enter special four-wheel drive vehicles, ordinary saloons and even motorcycles; before long a whole new form of racing was evolved. The best known of these races is the Baja 1000, a 1000-mile race down the rocky landscape of the Baja peninsular of California. The experts traverse the rough ground at fantastic speeds, the soft suspensions and high ground clearance enabling them to drive fast over boulders and gullies.

This type of racing is not possible in Europe because of the lack of suitable country, but other off-road sports are popular; these range from simple driving tests on any handy car park to autocross which is run on a

McLarens dominated the US Can-Am sports car series from 1968 until 1971. In 1972 turbocharged Porsches more than matched their speeds. Here Hulme leads McLaren team mate Revson

circuit laid out in any suitable grass field. A derivation of autocross is rallycross which uses part of a normal racing circuit and part of the infield so that drivers have to be experts at racing on tarmac and muddy grass. Works teams have often taken part in these televised spectaculars with Ford, British Leyland, Chrysler and DAF being well represented. Ford even developed a special four-wheel drive Capri for rallycross while DAF went so far as to mount a Ford twin camshaft BDA engine in the cockpit of a DAF next to the driver, the drive going to the four wheels via a DAF Variomatic belt drive automatic transmission.

Although motor racing and rallying has become almost an industry due to the vast amounts of money involved the competitive element is as strong as ever. However, there are signs that restrictions might well be placed on motor racing and rallying because of noise, pollution and interference with normal everyday life. Already motor racing is banned in Switzerland and determined attempts have been made to ban it in Sweden. The motor racing and rallying fraternity is well aware of this threat and is putting its own house in order by making circuits much safer, by improving fire fighting equipment, fitting drivers with special clothing and building safer cars, for the exhilaration and technical challenges of motor sport are irresistible.

SOME MOTORING FIRSTS

1770 The first vehicle moved by artificial power was made by Joseph Cugnot in France. Commissioned in 1769, it was steam powered.
1771 The first 'automotive' accident occurred when Cugnot's steam carriage hit a wall.
1824 The first car powered by an internal combustion engine (a 'gas-vacuum' device) was built by Samuel Brown in England.
1832 The first fatal motor accident occurred when a steam boiler exploded on one of Walter Hancock's buses.
1862 The first practicable car with an internal combustion engine was built by Etienne Lenoir.
1865 The first speed limits in England were imposed under the 'Red Flag Act'.
1887 The first 'production car', a Benz, was sold.
1894 The first motoring competition was the Paris-Rouen trial. The first American car was built by Charles and Frank Duryea.
1895 The first all-British car was the Lanchester designed by Frederick Lanchester. The first 'Motor Show' in Great Britain was held by Sir David Salomons. The first American 'motor competition', the Chicago Times-Herald contest, was held.
1896 The first four cylinder automotive engine was produced by Panhard et Levassor. The first electric self starter was used on an Arnold car in England. The first motor club in the world was the Automobile Club de France. The first motorists' association in Britain was the Motor Car Club.
1898 Acetylene burning headlamps came into use. The first lady racing driver, Madame Laumaille, took part in the Marseilles-Nice race.
1899 The first car to exceed 60 mph (a mile a minute) was the electric *Jamais Contente*, driven by Camille Jenatzy.
1901 The first race to carry the title Grand Prix was run at Pau.
1902 The first straight-eight engine was produced by Charron, Giradot and Voigt of Paris.
1903 The first six-cylinder car was produced by Spyker of Holland. The first driving licences were issued in Britain. The first car registration plates were issued in England.
1904 The first man to officially exceed 100 mph on land was Louis Rigolly, with a Gobron-Brillié.
1906 The first roadside petrol pump was set up in the USA. The first national Grand Prix, the French GP, was run at Le Mans, and won by Szisz, driving a Renault.

1907 The first supercharged automotive engine was built by Chadwick.
1908 The first American Grand Prix was run at Savannah, and won by Louis Wagner, driving a Fiat.
1909 The first four wheel braking system as a standard fitment was offered by Arrol-Johnston.
1911 The first Indianapolis 500-mile race was run, and won by Ray Harroun, driving a Marmon Wasp.
1915 The first mechanical (vacuum-operated) screen wiper was introduced by Willys-Knight.
1916 The first production V-12 was introduced by Packard.
1919 The first traffic light was installed in Detroit, USA.
1920 The first production straight-eight was introduced by Isotta-Fraschini.
1921 The first cars to be marketed in standard trim with a supercharger were the 6/25/40PS and 10/40/65PS Mercedes. The first radio set was fitted to a car.
1922 The first factory to produce a million cars in a year was Ford of America.
1923 The first Le Mans 24-hour race was run, and won by a Chenard et Walcker driven by Lagache and Léonard.
1924 The first motorway was opened, between Milan and Varese.
1926 The first British Grand Prix was run at Brooklands, and won by Louis Wagner and Robert Sénéchel, driving a Delage. The first oil pressure warning light was fitted, to a Talbot. The first Russian built private car in production was the Nami-I.
1927 The first rear axle to use hypoid bevel gears was the Packard. The first London-Brighton Commemoration run was staged. The first man to officially exceed 200 mph on land was Sir Henry Segrave, in the '1000 Horsepower' Sunbeam.
1929 The first car offered with a syncromesh gearbox was introduced by Cadillac.
1930 The first private car with a 16-cylinder engine was introduced by Bugatti.
1931 The first all-syncromesh gearbox was announced by the German firm of ZF.
1932 The first British cars to use syncromesh gearboxes were Vauxhall and Rolls-Royce.
1934 The first electrically operated convertible was fitted to a Peugeot. The first drive-in cinema was opened in Camden, New Jersey, USA. The first automobile overdrive was introduced by Chrysler. The first British production model to use automatic transmission was the 18 hp Austin.

1935 The first man to exceed 300 mph on land was Sir Malcolm Campbell in Bluebird. The first headlamp flashers were used on the Fiat 1500. The first stretch of German *autobahn* was opened, between Damstadt and Frankfurt. The first parking meter was used in Oklahoma City, USA. The first windscreen washers were introduced, by Triumph.
1936 The first retractable headlights were used on the Cord 810. The first diesel-engined private car to be marketed was the Mercedes-Benz 260D.
1938 The first racing car disc brakes were fitted to an Indianapolis Miller. The first car to be offered with air conditioning was a Nash.
1940 The first American dual-carriageway turnpike, the Pennsylvania Turnpike, was opened.
1945 The first post-war motor race took place, in Paris.
1947 The first man to officially exceed 400 mph on land was John Cobb, in his Napier-Railton.
1950 The world's first gas turbine powered passenger car was the Rover JET 1.
1953 The first production car with a glass fibre body was the Chevrolet Corvette. The first radial ply tyre was the Michelin X.
1957 The first British car to win a World Championship race was the Vanwall of Stirling Moss and Tony Brooks which won the British GP.
1958 The first British Motorway was opened (at Preston).
1961 The first British car to sell more than a million examples was the Morris Minor.
1962 The first car to use an overhead camshaft driven by a cogged belt was the Glas S1004. The first European factory to produce a million private cars in a year was Volkswagen.
1963 The first gas turbine engine racing car, a Rover-BRM, ran in a road race (the Le Mans 24-hour Race). The first car to use a rotary engine was the NSU Wankel Spyder.
1964 The first gas turbine powered passenger car to be used by the public was the Chrysler Turbo Dart. The first man to exceed 500 mph on land was Craig Breedlove in his three-wheeled jet-propelled *Spirit of America*
1965 The first man to exceed 600 mph on land was Craig Breedlove in his jet-propelled *Spirit of America Sonic I*.
1966 The first production road car to use four wheel drive was the Jensen FF.

Modern cockpits. *Right:*
Lamborghini Espada. *Below:*
Ferrari Dino.
Opposite top: de Tomaso Pantera.
Opposite bottom: Shelby American
Cobra.

INDEX